The Religious Thought of
H. RICHARD NIEBUHR

Jerry A. Irish

John Knox Press
ATLANTA

Library of Congress Cataloging in Publication Data

Irish, Jerry A., 1936–
    The religious thought of H. Richard Niebuhr.

    1. Niebuhr, H. Richard (Helmut Richard), 1894–1962.
I. Title.
BX4827.N47174   1983   230′.5734′0924   83–6202
ISBN 0–8042–0680–5

10 9 8 7 6 5 4 3 2 1
Printed in the United States of America
John Knox Press
Atlanta, Georgia 30365

ACKNOWLEDGMENTS

Unless otherwise indicated, Scripture quotations are from the Revised Standard Version of the Holy Bible, copyright, 1946, 1952, and © 1971, 1973 by the Division of Christian Education, National Council of the Churches of Christ in the U. S. A. and used by permission.

Acknowledgment is made for permission to quote from the following sources:

To Mrs. Florence M. Niebuhr for the following unpublished articles of H. Richard Niebuhr: "A Christian Interpretation of War," mimeographed, 1943; "The Church Defines Itself in the World," mimeographed, 1957; "Martin Luther and the Renewal of Human Confidence," typescript, 1959; "Towards New Symbols," transcription of tape recording of the Cole lectures, 1960.

To The Christian Century Foundation for excerpts from the following articles: "Reformation: Continuing Imperative" by H. Richard Niebuhr. Copyright 1960 Christian Century Foundation. Reprinted by permission from the March 2, 1960 issue of The Christian Century. "Back to Benedict?" by H. Richard Niebuhr. Copyright 1925 Christian Century Foundation. Reprinted by permission from the July 2, 1925 issue of The Christian Century. "Is God in the War?" by Virgil C. Aldrich and H. Richard Niebuhr. Copyright 1942 Christian Century Foundation. Reprinted by permission from the August 5, 1942 issue of The Christian Century. "War as Crucifixion" by H. Richard Niebuhr. Copyright 1943 Christian Century Foundation. Reprinted by permission from the April 28, 1943 issue of The Christian Century. "War as the Judgment of God" by H. Richard Niebuhr. Copyright 1942 Christian Century Foundation. Reprinted by permission from The Christian Century.

To Harper & Row, Publishers, Inc. for specified excerpts from the following: CHRIST AND CULTURE by H. Richard Niebuhr. Copyright, 1951, by Harper & Row, Publishers, Inc. RADICAL MONOTHEISM AND WESTERN CULTURE, with Supplementary Essays by H. Richard Niebuhr. Copyright 1943, 1952, © 1955, 1960 by H. Richard Niebuhr. THE RESPONSIBLE SELF by H. Richard Niebuhr. Copyright © 1963 by Florence M. Niebuhr. "The Responsibility of the Church for Society" by H. Richard Niebuhr in THE GOSPEL, THE CHURCH AND THE WORLD, edited by Kenneth Scott Latourette. Copyright, 1946, by Harper & Row, Publishers, Inc.

To Macmillan Publishing Co., Inc. for material from THE MEANING OF REVELATION. Reprinted with permission of Macmillan Publishing Co., Inc. from THE MEANING OF REVELATION by H. Richard Niebuhr. Copyright 1941 by Macmillan Publishing Co., Inc., renewed 1969 by Florence Niebuhr, Cynthia M. Niebuhr and Richard R. Niebuhr.

To UNIVERSITAS for material from "The Ethical Crisis" by H. Richard Niebuhr. The article appeared in UNIVERSITAS, Vol. II, No. 2, Spring 1964. Copyright 1964 by Virgil Jones.

To the University of Chicago Press for material from "Man the Sinner" by H. Richard Niebuhr in JOURNAL OF RELIGION, 15 (July 1935), pp. 278, by permission of the University of Chicago Press.

To
Pat and Jeff
my social companions

CONTENTS

INTRODUCTION

Who am I? What shall I do? How is faith in God possible? These are questions we must ask in this time of rapid, often chaotic, and frequently destructive change. These questions instruct us, though they reveal no conclusive answers. Honestly and persistently asked, these questions might take us beyond the threat of nuclear annihilation to a way of life that acknowledges evil without giving in to it. These are the questions that H. Richard Niebuhr asked in all of his life and work.

More than anything else, Niebuhr gave us a *way* of asking the basic questions. He described the search for self-understanding and guidance, the coming to faith in God, without denying the limits of that quest or the mystery of that trust. Though we know very little about Niebuhr's personal life, we do know he was unable to "look the other way." The lines that etched his brow provide a telling clue. Perhaps they began to appear in the terrifying emptiness he felt when two young boys, brothers and members of the church he pastored in St. Louis, drowned beneath the ice while camping with him. Surely those furrows deepened as he watched young American men dying in pursuit of unconditional surrender from the nation that had given birth to his own father and his mother's grandparents.

For those of us who never met Niebuhr, never participated in his seminars, never heard him lecture, it is enough to know that he asked his own questions doggedly and unflinchingly. In the absence of personal incidents and private observations, we are forced to look at Niebuhr's work as a window on our own lives, our own experiences with one another and with God. We must ask Niebuhr's questions for ourselves.

Niebuhr was born in Wright City, Missouri, on September 3, 1894. His father, Gustav, a minister of the German Evangelical Synod of North America, had immigrated from Germany at the age of seventeen. Niebuhr's mother, Lydia, was the daughter of a German-American pastor. German theology, Bible readings in Hebrew and Greek, and a rich appreciation for the fine arts characterized the home Niebuhr shared with his sister and two brothers. Like his older brother, Reinhold, Niebuhr attended Elmhurst College, Elmhurst, Illinois, and Eden Theological Seminary, St. Louis, Missouri. In 1916, after working for a year on the staff of a newspaper in Lincoln, Illinois, he was ordained and began serving as pastor of the Walnut Park Evangelical Church in St. Louis. Niebuhr conducted the church's first services in English, one of many steps he took to Americanize his denomination without compromising its unique piety. During this period Niebuhr earned a master's degree in history at Washington University, St. Louis.

Niebuhr began his teaching career at Eden Seminary in 1919. In 1920 he married Florence Marie Mittendorff. They had two children, Cynthia and Richard Reinhold. The latter, following in the family tradition, is a theologian at Harvard Divinity School. Niebuhr spent the years 1922–24 at Yale Divinity School where he earned a B.D. and a Ph.D. His doctoral dissertation was on Ernst Troeltsch's philosophy of religion.

In 1924, at the age of thirty, Niebuhr became president of Elmhurst College. During his presidency the college improved its financial situation and achieved full academic accreditation. In 1927 Niebuhr was back at Eden Seminary, serving as academic dean and chairing negotiations that eventually led his denomination to unite with the Reformed Church to become, in 1934, the Evangelical and Reformed Church. This body in turn became part of the United Church of Christ in 1957. Insights gained from the combination of sociological research and practical church reform are evident in Niebuhr's first book, *The Social Sources of Denominationalism*, published in 1929.

Niebuhr took a sabbatical leave from Eden to study in Germany during the spring and summer of 1930. It was during this period that Paul Tillich's work began to influence Niebuhr's own theological reflections. A month-long trip to Russia would also bear on Niebuhr's later assessments of Marxism. Upon his return to the United States Niebuhr was invited to join the faculty at Yale Divinity School. In the fall of 1931, after a final year at Eden, Niebuhr became associate professor of Christian ethics at Yale, where he continued to teach until his death on July 5, 1962.

It has been said that Niebuhr was a theologian's theologian. This may simply be a way of distinguishing him from his brother Reinhold, a much more public figure. More significantly, it may refer to the impact Niebuhr's brand of theological scholarship had on the numerous students who attended Yale during his thirty years on the faculty. Many of these students became professors or pastors themselves. While Niebuhr's influence may be evident in the substance of their teaching or preaching, it is most striking in the intellectual style they inherited from their mentor. John Godsey has written of Niebuhr's students that they were "caught up in the workings of a great mind and through this experience learned how to think for themselves."[1] Such a tribute to Niebuhr's teaching applies as well to his written work.

The present essay sets forth Niebuhr's theology as a coherent unit. It is systematic in a way his own writing is not. None of Niebuhr's individual books or articles sets forth his religious thought fully or in complete outline. Niebuhr himself did not choose one concept or one method as a systematic principle for the exposition of the Christian faith. There are recurrent themes and images, but they spring from a deeper source of coherence: Niebuhr's belief that all persons exist and move and have their being in God. In its selection and organization of materials and in its weighting of various ideas, therefore, this essay offers, of necessity, an interpretive exposition. Those who wish to trace the development of Niebuhr's work and speculate as to the primary influences on his thinking will find guidance for that task in the concluding bibliography.

Who am I? What shall I do? How is faith in God possible? These questions shape my presentation of Niebuhr's thought beginning with his analysis of selfhood (Chapter I.) The issues of personal integrity and empowerment arising from his definition of responsibility and faith provide the foci for an account of Jesus Christ, the central symbolic form in the Christian tradition (Chapter II). Niebuhr's understanding of God is set forth in terms of Jesus Christ as revelatory event, as organizing principle and transforming power (Chapter III). What Niebuhr describes as a permanent revolution of mind and heart initiated and sustained by revelation entails as well a revolutionary community of radical faith (Chapter IV).

CHAPTER I

Selfhood

Our examination of Niebuhr's thought begins with the self. This starting point enables us to test the adequacy of Niebuhr's position against our own experience. We can begin right where we are. This starting point also commends itself on the basis of Niebuhr's approach to theological issues. The problem of God is a human problem.

Niebuhr views human existence as complex relational interaction. We are "beings in the midst of a field of natural and social forces, acted upon and reacting, attracted and repelling."[1] Nature, society, ideas, feelings—all bear on one another in and through selves who eat and sleep, work and play, love and hate. We live in a world of happenings and becomings, movement and change that confounds exhaustive analysis from any one perspective. Domestic fashion, foreign economy, human rights, ecclesiastical organization, national politics—an action in one area sets off reactions in each of the others. Our world is a far cry from the serial simplicity of "the house that Jack built."

In probing the complexities of relational interaction, we seek knowledge of ourselves and guidance for our activities. In Niebuhr's analysis of this process three concepts stand out: social companions, responsibility, and faith.

SOCIAL COMPANIONS

The self is fundamentally social in the sense that "it is a being which not only knows itself in relation to other selves but exists as self only in that relation."[2] The significance of Niebuhr's claim is first seen in self-consciousness or reflexive selfhood, the capacity of the human subject to experience itself as object. The self is an "I" experiencing a "me." The self can know and evaluate its actions, even its own thoughts, now and in the past. The self can prejudge its own anticipated behavior. This capacity to watch ourselves in action and listen to ourselves in thought is so basic we take it for granted. Yet were it not for this self-contained distinction between participant and observer, the process of human decision, the manner of choosing among alternatives, would be radically different. Something as routine as navigating a car through rush-hour traffic or describing an event to a friend would be impossible if we could not transcend our immediate involvement, if we could not witness our own activity.

Niebuhr contends that self-reflexiveness is rooted in the individual's relations to other selves. The duality of self as subject and self as object is only real in the remembered, contemporary, or anticipated presence of at least one other. I become an object to myself by taking the position of the other, by seeing myself as others see me.

As a baseball shortstop I become proficient by learning my own moves in relation to those of the other infielders. I can only execute the double play if I have "taken the position" of the second baseman fielding a ground ball between first and second. Only if I "see myself" as the pitcher sees me, can I take the pickoff throw with a runner leading off second. Even the consciousness of my overall playing ability and my competitive spirit is mediated by my teammates.

The grounding of the self's "I-me" duality in social relations is nowhere more evident than in the activity we call "conscience." We all have those internal conversations in which we attempt to justify some action of ours to an other. These conversations are striking in their debate-like character and in our own identification with both parties. There is no doubt that the debate takes place within the self. The same being is both judge and accused. Yet it is through the mediation of an other that I represent myself to myself. Niebuhr argues that the "alter" in the "ego-alter" dialectic is not primarily an idea or a law. It is another self.

Niebuhr calls the other that mediates self-reflexiveness a *social companion*. The social companion in whose presence the self is reflexive is also a knower and an evaluator. We can only take the position of the other if the other has a position to be taken. In a manner reminiscent of Martin Buber's "I-Thou," Niebuhr claims for the self/social companion relation the reciprocity that facilitates self-reflexiveness. Carrying the comparison further, the "I-It" situation is not reflexive because it lacks this reciprocity. Awareness moves from subject to object without turning back upon the subject. One-way, outer-directed awareness is consciousness, not self-consciousness.

For Niebuhr the individual who avoids I-Thou relation fails to exercise genuine selfhood. We need not conjure up a desert island to illustrate his claim. Antipersonnel bombs are effective because the pilot does not see his victims as persons torn apart and maimed by metal fragments. He does not take the position of the other and thereby escapes seeing himself as a mutilator whose devastation far exceeds that of the criminal who wields a knife in some dark alley.

In developing the concept of social companion, Niebuhr recognizes that the I-Thou encounter itself takes place in a context of relations. The Thou or social companion displays some constancy in its interaction with other Thous as well as in its interaction with the self. We come to know a friend not simply as an isolated individual, but as a participant in a context that extends beyond our friendship. Patterns of behavior are established among the members of the community I and Thou share. "The social self is never a mere I-Thou self but an I-*You* self, responding to a Thou that is a member of an interacting community."[3] Niebuhr's concept of social companion includes this plurality of Thous. Reflexive life in relation to social companions is I-Thou, I-You existence.

> When the Thou is present to me as a knower, it is present as the one that knows not only me but at least one other; and it knows

> me as knowing not only the Thou but something besides it. This encounter of I and Thou takes place, as it were, always in the presence of a third, from which I and Thou are distinguished and to which they also respond.[4]

In the case of a single social companion, the third in relation to both I and Thou is at least one other Thou. This I-Thou-You or self/social companion complex is the elementary triadic form of social selfhood and a constituent in all the self's more complex relations. To summarize Niebuhr's position as developed to this point: the social self participates in numerous relations, each manifesting a triad formed by self, social companions, and the "third" of the particular relation in question.

Niebuhr employs triadic form as an abstract device for the exploration of social selfhood. He distinguishes between two basic triadic configurations in which the self and its social companions participate. Since one of these is most evident in the double relation to society and nature whereby we come to know natural events, it is called a *nature triad*. By "nature" Niebuhr refers to those actualities that we know but that apparently do not know us or themselves, that "large world of events and agencies that we regard as impersonal, as purely objective or thing-like in character."[5] When the third becomes the mediator of self-knowledge, the triadic situation is no longer "natural" in Niebuhr's sense.

The second basic triadic form, the *cause triad*, is one in which the third is an object or an objective to which the self is devoted. It may be another person, an institution, a program, or an ideal. Devotion to this cause relates the self to other devotees of the same cause. Thus a triad is formed in which self and social companions are loyal to one another by virtue of their loyalty to a common cause. Family, soccer team, union shop, garden club, political party, and nation exemplify this configuration.

The third in a cause triad displays characteristics that distinguish it from its counterpart in a nature triad. First, a cause is personal in the reflexive sense. It is a medium of self-knowledge and self-evaluation. To be sure, the self does not take the position of the cause in the same way it takes the position of another

self. The reciprocity of self and cause is mediated by persons
with whom the self identifies. The personal element here is the
same feature Niebuhr points to when he asserts that the demands of conscience are made by representative Thous, not by
an abstract other or an isolated Thou. The committed self is known
and evaluated by the cause to which it is committed, but this
self-knowledge and evaluation is mediated by social companions,
remembered, present, and anticipated.

The cause triad is exemplified in family relations. Sibling ri-
valry that flourishes within the family often disappears when
brothers and sisters perceive a threat from outside the family.
Parents often remain social companions beyond the time of any
deep love for one another simply "for the sake of the children."
In these cases the family is a focus of commitment, a third that
relates self and other as brother and sister, or mother and father.

A woman's self-understanding may develop in relation to her
sense of feminism as a cause. The influence of representative
women, members of the local community or figures on the national scene, is strengthened by and strengthens her commitment to the liberation of women and men from discrimination
associated with gender. The mediators of female identity and
loyalty must compete with representatives of other causes that
may also provide a strong sense of self, but in relation to a different set of social companions. Accomplishment in the realm of
scholarship or success in the business world are alternative foci
for a woman's self-knowledge and self-evaluation.

A second feature of the cause that distinguishes it from the
third in a nature triad is its reference to something beyond itself.
Individuals who represent family commitment or feminist loyalty point beyond their particular community to its cause. "They
represent not the community only but what the community stands
for."[6] In the family the child learns basic attitudes toward persons
in the larger community. Honesty between parent and child represents on a small scale what is to be sought in all one's relations.
The solidarity called for by feminists is finally in the name of all
oppressed persons, be they women or men.

A third feature of cause triads is that they are often overlapping and cross-purposing. Competing claims operate within groups and between them. It would be quite enough to weigh the political claims of my nation upon myself and upon other nations. But this cannot be done in isolation from familial, vocational, and religious claims. I must be a father, teacher, churchman, and citizen all at once. Each of these roles is the personal focus on a network of relations among Thous. My social companions in one enterprise may appear as Its in light of some other cause to which I am committed. The causes themselves are unstable, their relevance and ranking varying from situation to situation. In politics, for instance, professional, party, and economic allegiances bring together individuals who may otherwise never associate with one another.

There is also movement in the realm of personal commitment. If the third in the self/social companion/cause triad points beyond itself to another cause, then a new triad is formed with a different constituency of social companions. If the patriot's representative figures appeal to liberty in calling for national allegiance, then the patriot may join forces with liberty-seeking persons from other nations. Consequently the patriot may be separated from some fellow-citizens and united with others. There will also be some different faces among the group of representative Thous who now mediate the patriot's self-knowledge. This movement among causes involves the self in a progression of judgments that gives it some independence from its immediate social relations. When the third in a cause triad no longer points beyond itself, the adherents to that cause constitute the final court of appeal in self-judgment. If, for example, the ultimate cause is the nation, some of the self's relations with foreign nationalists may be called into question by fellow-patriots who interpret such relations as treasonous.

Whether a triadic relation is of the nature or the cause variety is not determined solely by the third in question. The interest or disposition of the related selves may be the determining factor. An object of scientific study functions as a nonreflexive It, but it is not necessarily impersonal in itself. Political scientists make impersonal studies of nations to which patriots are passionately committed. Physiological studies are made of human beings who are also loved ones. Moreover, the same selves and social companions may be mutually related to natural objects and to causes simultaneously. Niebuhr's distinction between the two kinds of triadic relations is best stated in terms of the character of the total relationship, and neither kind of triad can be ignored. The self always stands in the natural world and in a society of selves with all its claims and allegiances.

Niebuhr's understanding of time illustrates the significance of social companions and their triadic relations. He describes the self's temporal situation in terms of *compresent* others and events, others and events that are present *with* the self. In order for the other, the not-myself, to influence my relations, it must be present still, now, or already. Self-existence is social-temporal existence.

We are most conscious of ourselves in the present when we confront others or events that are striking in their newness or dissimilarity to previous encounters. Some of us are off to work each day by eight, home again by six, day after day, week after week. Then there is that morning when a new department head announces a twenty percent cutback in personnel or that coffee break when acquaintance begins to blossom into friendship.

Our past is also a history of compresent others. Insofar as we carry the past with us, the others compresent then are compresent now in vivid memory or in repression. We remember our parents acting and reacting to us in anger and in love. We see again the stooped shoulders of the surgeon telling us he can do no more to heal our little boy. Our peculiar language and mannerisms manifest the compresence of friends and family further back than our memory can reach. And there are those sudden emotional reactions that we can only guess must have their origin in some past encounter echoing in the present. However clear or hazy, the past that is present must include that to which the self was related if it is to include the self at all.

The future is present in the self's anticipated relations. If the expected compresent others are part of a familiar routine, they have little impact at the moment. But how rich the present is when we are expecting the return of a loved one long absent.

And who has not experienced those exhilarating, panicky nows when some important information—the results of an examination, the winner of an election, the verdict of a jury—is about to be announced?

Time is a fundamental dimension of selfhood because the relational interaction of the social self is continuous. Memory and anticipation are acknowledgments that the relations in which the self is currently participating grew out of previous relations and will themselves develop into new relations. Were it not for the continuous interaction that the temporal dimension seeks to articulate, none of the systems or patterns of constancy that facilitate self-reflexiveness would ever emerge. Self-identity would be a meaningless action.

The social self's relations in the present extend into the past and the future. In this sense time is a condition of self-identity and self-understanding. *The self is in time.* But the relevance and impact of past and future compresences is also influenced by the self's present relations to its own particular compresent others. In this sense time is conditioned by self-identity and self-understanding. *Time is in the self.* Past and future are extensions of the present; the present is always rooted in a self.

The social-temporal dimensions that run throughout relational selfhood do not account for the self's presence in a particular society and time—why I *am* and why I am *I*. If the self pursues these matters far enough, it discovers its absolute dependence, its relation to the radical action whereby it has its being and has it in this society and time. The action is radical in that it cannot be identified with any relation or system of interaction within the social-temporal dimensions of selfhood. Faced with this conundrum, the self recognizes its most primitive relation, its relation to "the creative and destructive power, whence all things come and to which they all must return."[7]

The whence and whither of our being here and now seems an impenetrable mystery. Is it an alien power or a positive force? Is it simply fate, or nothing? For the moment we can identify it only as the one beyond the many, the final reality, the abyss we confront when we ask how it is that we have life and have it here and now.

When the self stands in relation to this last reality, it stands in relation to all other beings. All existents are members of this triad, and so the extent of the self's social companions in this relationship is universal. It may be that in relation to this third the self has its unity and its uniqueness. But Niebuhr points out how readily we ignore this other and the central self it reveals. The childhood question, "Why am I?" becomes "Why is humanity?" or, even more abstract, "What is a rational creature?"

To ignore the question of our identity in the ultimate context of being and time is to stand in relation to the one beyond the many societies and times much as we stand in relation to the third in a nature triad. We understand this other as nonreflexive, impersonal in its regard for the beings that pass before it. To ask the ultimate question, to seek the final boundary of our social-temporal existence, apparently adds nothing to our self-knowledge.

It might also be possible to stand in relation to the last reality as the third in a cause triad. Reaching the end of the movement through causes that point beyond themselves, the self might be related to the ultimate other as a personal force that is not indifferent to the state of the universe. Whether the final reality were demonic or gracious, whether its concern were best characterized as death-dealing or life-giving, would be another matter. But in either case, as a reflective cause it would influence the self's relations with its social companions. As personal, the object of the self's absolute dependence would affect all the self's relations in being and time.

RESPONSIBILITY

"Who am I?" "What shall I do?" Given the complexity of relational selfhood, these are hard questions to answer. Is there a central agency in the midst of our continual multi-dimensional activity, and if so, how does it find its bearings? How does the social, temporal, absolutely dependent self come to grips with its identity and organize its relations so as to act with integrity?

Niebuhr contends that symbols play a crucial role in our interaction with the world around us. Simultaneously emerging from and shaping our experience, symbols are the vehicles of meaning in the relation between knower and known. In the operation of symbols or images in self-understanding and guidance, a pattern notably present in a particular experience is often employed in the analysis of all experience. Niebuhr's own theory of responsibility is rooted in the image of men and women as answerers, persons responding to one another in dialogue.

Niebuhr prefers the imagery of *answerer* to that of *maker* or *citizen*. He finds responsiveness a more instructive clue than purposiveness or duty in coming to grips with the complex relational interaction that characterizes human existence. "What is going on?" more adequately poses the fundamental question of our lives as agents than "What is the goal to be achieved?" or "What is the law to be obeyed?" For the answerer, the focal point of human interaction is not primarily the good or the right but the fitting.

The theory of responsibility abstractly defined is "the idea of an agent's action as response to an action upon him in accordance with his interpretation of the latter action and with his expectation of response to his response; and all of this is in a continuing community of agents."[8] We can unpack this definition and identify four fairly distinct elements: response, interpretation, accountability, and social solidarity.

Response. "All life has the character of responsiveness."[9] This assertion is consistent with Niebuhr's organismic view of relational being. The responsiveness of moral acts is a consequence of the self's existence in the midst of complex relational interaction. As selves we always stand among social companions, remembered, present, or anticipated, not to mention our inescapable dependence upon the natural environment. No self-action can be initiated completely "out of context." Our acts are in response to actions upon us.

"What is going on?" Persistently and honestly asked, this question can be revealing under many different circumstances. To what am I responding when I punish my disobedient son? Is

the issue simply one of broken rules, or is the rebellion connected with our recent move to a new community? Perhaps I am
only responding to part of the situation when I isolate the breach
in discipline from the presence of an antagonistic sibling. Or am
I responding to my own frustration over a management problem
that continues to plague my department?

To what am I responding when I back a proposal for subsidized housing in my town? Is the plan designed in response to
an inequitable distribution of services in the community or the
economic interests of an enterprising developer? Will the housing site allow for adequate educational facilities, or does it simply
preserve the present homogeneity of my own school district? Is
my response to the real needs of other persons or the bad pub-
licity my community has been receiving?

In addition to pointing out the responsive character of self-
action and the plurality of forces that precipitate such action, the
question "What is going on?" makes the self aware of the social
nature of the situation in which it acts. A father's relation to his
son exists in the midst of family, community, and vocational relations. Response to ideals such as the availability of adequate
housing cannot be dissociated from response to personal goals of
wealth and comfort dictated by the dominant society. What is
happening is never happening to the self as an atomic individual.
How do we want to bring up our children in the midst of the
compelling but often conflicting models we see in our variety of
social relations? Can we find a creative response to the needs of
the disadvantaged in our community when the responses of our
friends are so varied?

As the question "What is going on?" makes the self sensitive
to the rich texture of a situation, it also brings to awareness the
givenness of that situation. It calls our attention to all those others and events over whose compresence we have no control. My
son has in fact been disobedient, and that disobedience remains
an issue whether or not I am presently disposed to deal with the
problem rationally. The disparities in housing, employment, and
education in my community are really there no matter how difficult or distasteful the proposals for their remedy.

Response analysis, with its sensitivity to the numerous forces acting on the self and its recognition of the real limits defined by these forces, can exert a debilitating influence on positive self-action. The disclosure of the given character of a situation can lead to personal capitulation in the face of fate; heightened sensitivity to the complexity of human existence can paralyze the self. Many housewives have watched their dreams and aspirations suffocated by the role expectations of their social companions; others have broken through those role expectations only to be overwhelmed by the possibilities of the new situation. Such consequences point up the crucial importance of the second element in Niebuhr's responsibility theory.

Interpretation. If response tends to emphasize the givenness of human existence, interpretation suggests the element of freedom. Interpretation represents the subjective side of the question "What is going on?" Here the host of forces impinging upon the self is organized for meaning. Here the sensitive self relates its data and puts individual factors into larger contexts. How this is done bears heavily on the response.

The meaning of a child's disobedience is one thing if only the child, his parents, and a broken rule are taken into consideration. The meaning may be quite different if the child's peers, teachers, siblings, and physiological or psychological development are considered. How the father relates all these factors will influence his action. The extension of the scene he surveys and the manner in which he organizes the components of that scene are points at which he exercises freedom in determining what responsive action to take. Even if he decides not to act at all in the face of complexity, he has made an interpretation. He understands the situation between himself and his disobedient child to be hopeless so far as any specific measures of his own are concerned. In this sense his decision to do nothing is a free act.

It would be a misinterpretation of Niebuhr's responsibility theory to suggest that the interpretive element is really an argument for making all our responses to action upon us in the largest possible context. While it is certainly the case that the extension of the relational context in which one stands may reveal important considerations, interpretation may also involve a narrowing of perspective. Our responses to social issues such as racism, war, and pollution may become fitting only when we base our interpretation on an assessment of our immediate relations. Sometimes grand interpretations having to do with national priorities, political ideologies, and theological world views shield us from the day-to-day responses that constitute our identity as persons. Niebuhr's response analysis is perverted into a clever evasion if we neglect the objective clause in his question "What is happening to me?" How I interpret the housing patterns in my community and how I participate in their preservation or change may be far more telling than my professed "position on subsidized housing."

The freedom that interpretation brings to self-action is not limited to those cases in which the respondent can actually alter the external circumstances. The most striking examples of interpretive freedom and its consequences in the midst of unchanging circumstances are seen in conjunction with human suffering. The stories that have survived our twentieth-century death camps and refugee compounds reveal the significance of the self's interpretation of events it cannot control. A similar drama is enacted daily in the hospitals and homes of the permanently maimed and diseased. As Niebuhr writes:

> . . . it is in the response to suffering that many and perhaps all men, individually and in their groups, define themselves, take on character, develop their ethos. And their responses are functions of their interpretation of what is happening to them as well as of the action upon them.[10]

The interpretive process of relating persons and events with one another in contexts that have a meaning of their own is not arbitrary. The social self is always making its interpretations in the presence of companions, remembered, contemporary, or anticipated. Nevertheless, there are usually significant interpretive options that allow some degree of individual freedom. Inherited categories and patterns of interpretation can themselves be modified. The organization of material into new meaning complexes has been practiced with dramatic results by professional historians and psychotherapists, not to mention lay persons who must reinterpret their past in order to make sense out of what is happening to them in the present. So too, the reinterpretation of anticipated events often alters our response to present happenings.

The element of interpretation in response analysis also allows for consideration of the good and the right. Our understanding of a friend's goals and ideals will influence our response to the favors asked and the commitments made by that friend. Our nation's response to a foreign power's treaty proposals will involve judgments as to that power's respect for human justice and international law. One of the merits of asking what is going on rather than what is good or what is right in a particular situation is precisely this sensitivity to the value scales and notions of duty held by other parties to whom we are related.

Accountability. The third element in responsibility theory calls attention to the forward-looking character of fitting action. "Our actions are responsible not only insofar as they are reactions to interpreted actions upon us but also insofar as they are made in anticipation of answers to our answers."[11] Since the relational activity in which the self participates is continual, the fitting act, like a statement in a dialogue, takes its place in a total conversation with a meaning of its own.

Accountability also points to the factor of evaluation in responsible action. Given our anticipation of reactions to our response, some responses seem more fitting than others. The appropriateness of a response depends upon the continuing dialogue of which it is a part. But this raises the prior question of the self's interpretation of the situation, and we see that the four elements of responsibility theory are interrelated. Each refers to part of an integrated response pattern of self-agency. Response, interpretation, accountability, and social solidarity are abstractions intended to call attention to what goes on in responsible self-conduct. The terms are functions of one another, not distinct chronological steps taken on the way to a fitting act.

When the self anticipates reactions to its response, it is defining the meaning of the act to which it is responding and the relevant extent of the relations that constitute that meaning. Accountability is another way of posing the question "To whom or what am I responding and in what context?" When responsibility theory is used as an instrument of analysis, accountability identifies the self's expectation of reactions to its own response and the sense of judgment implied in that expectation. We often anticipate the future in terms of representative Thous. Always in the midst of social companions, our questions of accountability tend to be couched in the personal mode. "To whom do I appeal to sanction my response?" "Who will judge the reactions precipitated by my response?" The answers to such questions define the realm in which accountability is a consideration. What the self is responsible *for* depends upon whom the self is responsible *to*. We shall see that the patterns of meaning and the networks of interactional continuity that provide links between present response and anticipated reaction exhibit the triadic structure we discovered in our analysis of social companions.

To whom am I accountable when I deal with my disobedient son? If the assessment I value most is that of my wife, then the reactions I look forward to in determining my present action will probably be limited to the immediate family. How will my other children respond to the action I take? Questions of accountability may lead me beyond the family: "What will the neighbors think?" I may even have to assess my accountability before the law. With the spread of illegal alcohol and drug use, parents move to yet another context in asking to whom they are accountable in dealing with the actions of their children.

To whom am I accountable in my response to social issues such as subsidized housing in my neighborhood? The answer may be evident in terms of the groups in which I participate. Am I a member of the homeowners' association that is trying to preserve the community just as it stands? Have I joined the concerned parents' group that wants a new elementary school to accommodate the influx of low-income families, or do I prefer the school board plan which would expand present elementary school facilities so as to accommodate the new children on an integrated basis? And what are the consequences I anticipate for my own children? Will I remain in the community or move farther out of town?

We must be careful at this point not to make a superficial equation between accountability in Niebuhr's responsibility model and commitment to a cause in his analysis of relational selfhood. The object of commitment and that to which the self is accountable in a particular situation may coincide, but we are working with two sets of abstractions here. If we wish to put the matter of accountability in terms of the cause triad manifest in relational selfhood, we might say that mere responsiveness becomes responsibility when the self recognizes and seeks to act upon its accountability before a reflective third or a mediating jury of representative Thous, social companions committed to the same cause. When I anticipate the consequences of my response in a particular situation, I may not be making a self-conscious analysis of my commitments. But surely the range of consequences that matter to me and the particular effects I would like to realize say something about my companions and the causes to which we are committed.

Social solidarity. The temporal extension of personal interaction that raises the question of accountability is matched by an extension in being that raises the question of social solidarity. This fourth element in Niebuhr's responsibility theory refers to the substantial continuity in the agency of selves and communities that is the basis of responsible rather than merely responsive action. In being accountable, in anticipating reactions to its own response, the self assumes some constancy in its own self-agency and that of other selves. It acts as if there were a connectedness in being. The self in society, the self in time, and the self in absolute dependence is the self in various dimensions of its connectedness.

Responsive interpretation attempts to discover the real connections among things, what is actually going on. Accountability pursues these connections into the future, assuming a continuity in time as well as a solidarity in being. Insofar as social solidarity is a report of experience, it calls our attention to a basic assumption in all our efforts at self-understanding and guidance. The self is in a context; it is part of a whole. Insofar as social solidarity serves as an instrument of analysis, it probes the extent of that context, the dimensions of that whole.

If I limit the interpretation of my son's disobedience to the rebellious act alone, my response will be fitting in a set of connections that is only part of the total scene. If I anticipate only the reaction of other members of the family to my response, I may fracture my son's equally important relations with his peers. The nature of the relation that has existed between me and my own parents is another factor in the responses I make to my children.

What connections are there between my activities and the poor in my community? Does my income depend upon their labor or their consumption? Do my social and political endeavors increase or decrease the accessibility of employment and recreational facilities for the poor? Is my solidarity with the dispossessed characterized by compassion for them or fear for my own possessions?

As a theme, social solidarity gives expression to the pressure of the actual situation on the self's interpretation and sense of accountability. In order for a response to be fitting, it must fit what is actually going on. If the interpretation of an act upon the self takes that act out of its context or fails to see fully the significant extent of that context, then the response is bound to be distorted or partial. We can also see that the social companions a self has by virtue of its commitment to a cause are not necessarily the only beings with which the self stands in social solidarity. Though I may be committed to a particular course of action with respect to my son's disobedience and stand with other parents in that commitment, I am also living in a neighborhood with parents who may not share that commitment.

Enthusiastic commitments to a narrow cause may blind the self to important elements in its relational being or force it to deny those elements. My desire to preserve the present configuration of my suburban neighborhood may preclude my recognition of possibilities that might actually improve upon the situation. It may even bring me into defensive conflict with persons who would otherwise be my friends.

The divisiveness that shows up when the self is accountable to a limited cause is the negative counterpart of the transcendent reference of thirds in cause triads. The movement to a third beyond each third is directed toward an inclusive interpretation of the full range of social solidarity. It is a movement in the direction of a universal cause that would integrate the action of all selves. Before such a cause the self would be accountable for all its responses. It would seek to anticipate the consequences of its action on as wide a scale as possible. It would be responsible in a universal context of social solidarity. Responsibility theory and the self/social companion/cause triad come into closer identity as one approaches universal responsibility and ultimate commitment.

Niebuhr's responsibility theory is an adequate report of experience and an instructive instrument of analysis. Used as a guide in self-determination, however, it only directs; it does not decide. While it calls attention to the move from responsiveness to responsibility, it does not tell the self to whom or what it is actually accountable. It points out but does not erase the discrepancy between one's social companions and the full extent of social solidarity. It suggests that self-integrity might be found in relation to a cause that holds the self accountable in all its other relations, but it does not identify that cause. If it is to do more than reveal the intricacies of human agency, responsibility theory with its symbolism of the answerer must be coupled with an organizing principle, a figure that can give content to the responsible life.

FAITH

In exploring the salient features of relational selfhood and distinguishing among important elements in responsible self-conduct, we have recognized the significance of interpersonal commitment among social companions. Niebuhr's understanding of faith builds on this recognition. He defines *faith* as trust and loyalty, focusing on its interpersonal meaning as distinct from its cognitive usage. Faith is "a fundamental personal attitude . . . apparently universal or general enough to be widely recognized . . . the attitude and action of confidence in, and fidelity to, certain realities as the sources of value and the objects of loyalty."[12]

As *trust*, faith is reliance upon a source and center of value. I trust my friend because my friend values me and, I am confident, will continue to do so. I need not be wary of betrayal or deception. More than this, I have worth and so too do my actions because of my friend's evaluation. As long as I have such a friend, my life is meaningful; my deeds have purpose.

As *loyalty*, faith is commitment and devotion to a cause. If I am a faithful friend, I am not only trusting but trustworthy. I value my friend and seek ways of promoting my friend's well-being. If trust is taken as the passive element in faith, then loyalty is its active component.

"Center of value" and "cause" designate two facets of the same object of faith. My friend values me and my activity; at the same time I see my friend's best interests as a cause to be served.

There is another element in the composition of the faith relationship understood in an interpersonal sense. I can sometimes distinguish between my friend and our common cause. Perhaps this cause is the friendship itself. There are times when we act to preserve a relationship that has meaning and value of its own. True friends are able to absorb the occasional unfriendly acts of their partners out of a trust in and allegiance to the friendship as well as the friend. Then again, the common cause may be something that transcends the friendship. Such a cause may provide the initial basis for the friendship and perhaps even its continuing sustenance. Common causes such as political power, nationalism, and civil rights have spawned friendships between many an unlikely pair.

As a social bond of mutual trust and loyalty in relation to a value-center and cause, faith manifests the triadic form in which the third is both reflexive and self-transcendent. Faith has its vitality in a double movement among self, social companion, and cause.

> I trust the companion in his loyalty to me, and in his loyalty to the cause to which I am also trying to be faithful. I expect his

trust in me as one who will not only never let him down but as one who will not let down the cause and then I somehow try to trust the cause, that which transcends us both as that which will not let him down or deceive him and which will not deceive me or let me down. Here is at least a kind of triad of faith.[13]

When dealing with faith simply as that personal attitude of trust and loyalty that characterizes much of our social interaction, there is little reason to distinguish it from the general triadic form of social relations constituted by self, social companions, and cause. However, there is reason to make a distinction when the object of faith is *the* cause. Niebuhr's primary focus is on those faith triads that qualify all the rest. The faith triad that has the most profound significance for a self is the one that is constituted by that self, its final cause, and its primary community of social companions.

To have such faith, the faith that life is worth living, is, according to Niebuhr, to have a god. In acting as though life were meaningful, we are relying on something that makes it so; that "something" is our god. Thus Niebuhr speaks of the "apparently universal human necessity of faith and of the inescapability of its gods, not as supernatural beings but as value-centers and objects of devotion."[14] The gods are the objects of our ultimate trust and loyalty.

Faith is always attached to an object. The gods are the objective realities to which the subjective activity of faith is directed. Faith and the gods belong together. Niebuhr is fond of quoting Luther on this matter: "Trust and faith of the heart alone make both God and idol. . . . For the two, faith and God, hold close together. Whatever then thy heart clings to . . . and relies upon, that is properly thy God."[15]

To have faith is to have a god. So it is that the forms of faith are properly called "theisms." The three basic theistic configurations of trust and loyalty constitute an abstract typology. Niebuhr points out that their concrete embodiment in persons and communities is always marked by ambiguity.

Henotheism is faith in one god among many. As Niebuhr describes it, the henotheistic form of faith has as its center of value and object of devotion a finite society. Any social unit can qualify as a god of henotheistic faith so long as it is a community from which one can derive one's value and to which one can commit one's service.

Nationalism manifests the henotheistic form of faith as clearly as it will be found anywhere. The survival and prosperity of the nation are the final tests of any activity on the part of the citizens. "My country, right or wrong" and "America, love it or leave it" are henotheistic slogans. Industry, art, religion, and education stand under a national evaluation that is itself beyond question. National boundaries determine the definition of friend and foe; national interests determine the definition of ally and enemy. In nationalism, as in all examples of henotheism, something is left out. The horizon of the closed society is always less than universal.

Niebuhr cites Marxism as a nonnationalist example of henotheism. Here the center of value is the international community of the proletariat, and the cause is the class struggle. Marxism, more inclusive than nationalism, is still a closed society. These two "isms" are pitted against one another around the world. If we doubt the degree of trust and loyalty generated by such gods, we need only review the history of anticommunism in the United States with its henotheistic motto "Better dead than red." Or we can review the bloody history of "world communism" in Eastern Europe and elsewhere.

Polytheism is the simultaneous or successive faith in many gods. It is characterized by multiple sources of meaning and a proliferation of commitments. Polytheism sustains no enduring community in which the self is assured of worth. The polytheist tries to find meaning in a variety of entities and enterprises and usually ends up serving a number of limited causes at the same time.

Niebuhr observes that polytheism with its multiple value centers and causes generally follows the dissolution of henotheistic faith, the loss of confidence in a closed society such as the nation. In the wake of two world wars and one political or economic crisis after another, in the midst of increasing poverty and pollution, not to mention a tragic war in Southeast Asia and a nuclear arms race that numbs the imagination, one might expect to find the polytheism Niebuhr describes.

In the United States there does seem to be a plethora of value centers and a pluralism of causes. Increased affluence and leisure, for some at least, have matched social disillusionment with a wide variety of meaning-givers. Whether one gets one's sense of worth from increasing wealth, or playing the guitar, or pruning roses, or reaching orgasm, or being sensitive in a small group, one finds oneself in the midst of allied devotees who publish shelves of manuals and tracts, promote conferences and institutes, and send out missionaries with introductory offers. Whether one gives one's loyalty to the Democratic party or women's liberation or the American Rifle Association or Yale University or little league baseball, one finds oneself in the midst of allied workers who are equally concerned and who have already developed a program and budget for the next decade.

Those of us who are polytheists have decided to worship and work in several communities, either simultaneously or serially. The situation is hectic. Husbands and wives see one another between meetings. Children get car sick traveling from one activity to the next. Some families have taken up camping as a way of getting together for a week or two each year. It may well be that the self cannot survive this pace. Perhaps the solution will be a kind of social suicide in which we gradually become oblivious to the enigma of our own identity. It is not uncommon for the active polytheist to be apathetic with respect to personal or national destiny, to ignore the problem of individual or environmental death. The polytheist is internally divided, pulled hither and yon until wearied of even trying to get it all together.

Radical monotheism is faith in one beyond the many. It is universal trust matched with universal loyalty. As its center of value, radical monotheism substitutes for the closed society of henotheism the principle of being itself. As its cause, radical monotheism substitutes for the numerous meaning-givers of polytheism the principle of value. Radical monotheism relies on the source and sustainer of being for the value of the self and all other existents. The principle of being and the principle of value are identical. Since all being participates in the same one that is the center of value, whatever is, is good.

Through trust in the universal principle of being, the radically monotheistic self is related to all other beings in the universe. Its cause is at once the principle of being and the entire realm of being. The unity of the realm of being is due not only to the loyalty of one existent to the other, but to the transcendent loyalty of the sustainer of all existents. So it is that the universal loyalty of radical monotheism is directed toward each being and toward the universal community in which it participates. For the radical monotheist, one's neighbor is one's "companion in being."[16]

Niebuhr refers to the god of radical monotheism as the principle of being and the principle of value rather than the highest being and the highest value, or Being and the Good. The one by reference to which all things have their being and value is not itself a being or a value in the usual sense. In Niebuhr's own writing this object of radically monotheistic faith is indicated by capitalizing the initial letter of the words "one" and "god." The God of radical monotheism is the One beyond the many, the One in relation to which all things have their value.

Niebuhr's abstract concept of radical monotheism is not a theory on which faith can stand. Nor is it intended as an argument for the existence of God. The ultimate identification of being and value in radical monotheism is "a point of departure and not a deduction."[17] Niebuhr's analysis of this form of faith does not assume the priority of being or value, and radical monotheism itself does not wait upon the development of a convincing theory about the existence or worth of its object.

Niebuhr associates the historical appearance of radical monotheism with such figures as Moses, the great prophets of Israel, and Jesus Christ. In such persons we find "the concrete expression in a total human life of radical trust in the One and of universal loyalty to the realm of being."[18] At some stages in the life of Israel or in Western civilization's medieval synthesis or sixteenth-century Reformation we may discover the corporate manifestation of radical faith. Whether in an individual or in a community, the presence of such trust in and loyalty to the One beyond the many pervades all the activities and provinces of life and culture. But radical monotheism, like henotheism and polytheism, is seldom, if ever, purely embodied. Nor is its competition with the other two forms of faith limited to religious practices and institutions.

The mutually modifying struggle among the forms of faith is evident in the political community. Our previous references to nationalism as a manifestation of henotheistic faith may suggest a characterization that is too simple. Undoubtedly many nations have so blurred the distinction between themselves and their transcendent cause that a nationalistic faith has absorbed a henotheistic faith more broadly conceived. The United States' national self-interest has often supplanted the cause of "freedom-loving peoples everywhere" in practice if not in political rhetoric. Nonetheless, there is a continual thrust of monotheism that never lets the exclusive faith of the national community rest. The realm of human being is not limited to persons with white skin; the realm of nature is not divided according to territorial treaties; the quality of human life is not defined by the gross national product. Insofar as it is present in persons and communities, radical monotheism attacks these exclusive limits, divisions, and definitions.

> It will not do, to be sure, to say that the American nation is intensely God-fearing in a monotheistic sense of God; there is too much evidence to the contrary. Yet God-fearingness, as reverence for the principle of all being and for its domain, is present among us and is in almost daily conflict or tension with our large and small social faiths.[19]

Though none of the forms of faith is to be found purely embodied in any one individual or group, they are to be found in various stages of ascendancy in all individuals and groups. Henotheism offers integrated selfhood through enduring and meaningful community, but sooner or later it excludes some other community, some other aspect or dimension of the realm of being. Polytheism with its plurality of value-centers and causes may not be exclusive, but the price of its kind of inclusiveness is the loss of self-integrity. Radical monotheism pushes beyond each exclusive realm of the henotheist towards a universal community. It recognizes the real merits of the gods of polytheism in the midst of a rich relational context. "Radical monotheism dethrones all absolutes short of the principle of being itself. At the same time it reverences every relative existent."[20]

In the complex relational interaction that is human existence, the self may stand in numerous triadic contexts characterized by mutual trust and loyalty. Movement and tension are apparent in and among these communities of interpersonal faith. Responsible action in one such context may be irresponsible in another. And there is no guarantee that one's social companions in faith correspond to one's actual companions in being and time. But Niebuhr contends that the self always stands in one triad of faith whereby it seeks to order all its other relations of trust and loyalty, even if only momentarily as in polytheism. Herein lies the significance of the theistic forms of faith. Henotheism, polytheism, and radical monotheism are special instances of the cause triad because they refer to the self in its most fundamental confidence and loyalty. The objects of theistic faith are the final centers of value and the ultimate causes. They are the gods. For their devotees they mark the end of the movement through self-transcending thirds. They must bestow meaning when all else fails.

Many of the gods to which we attach our faith cannot support meaningful existence in the face of crisis or even through the round of common daily affairs. Such gods cannot satisfy what Niebuhr calls our religious need, the need for that which makes life worth living. The question of religious need is not whether a god exists but rather what being or beings have the value of deity. What object or objects of faith support a meaningful context for any set of circumstances? Expressed in terms of responsibility theory, the question is what center of value and cause provides a sufficient focus for all our interpretations and an adequate community of faithful social companions before whom we stand in all our accountability.

The religious question can also be understood as the struggle among various forms of faith to facilitate self-identity and integrity of action. Polytheistic and henotheistic faiths are frustrating and divisive. Their partial centers of value always leave out important elements of experience; their exclusive causes fail to integrate all the self's responses. The movement through self-transcending thirds characteristic of cause triads is seen here as a tension that seeks resolution in the direction of universal faith. The drive to radical monotheism is the last phase, or better, the pervasive force in the movement through thirds that point beyond themselves. The ultimate cause short of which all causes are limited is the object of radical monotheism. It is the One beyond the many, the source, sustenance, and end of all being, the inscrutable power upon which the self is absolutely dependent.

If the object of faith were only a cause in the strictest sense, that is only an object of loyalty, then perhaps the self could pledge its allegiance to the One beyond the many simply by taking courage. But the object of faith is also a center of value, a cause that is trusted. Faith is confidence, as well as loyalty, and neither element can exist by itself. Radical monotheism is radical faith not simply because its cause is the principle of being but because that cause is also its center of value. Radical monotheism rests its confidence in that last reality before which all things must pass.

How can the principle of being, the mysterious action by which *I am I*, be the one in which I place my confidence? How can a self trust the void at the limits of its existence? How can it say "God" to the slayer of all its gods? How can that which raises the question of meaning most starkly be the answer? The religious question, and with it the problem of self-identity, is how faith in the One beyond the many is possible. The movement of ultimate trust and loyalty from the gods to the God of radical monotheism requires a transforming power.

CHAPTER II

Jesus Christ

Niebuhr's analysis of selfhood discloses the complex relational interaction that characterizes human existence. His picture of the responsible, faithful self defines the quest for self-understanding and guidance in terms of an organizing principle for the direction of response analysis and a transforming power for the radicalization of faith. For Niebuhr this quest is answered in Jesus Christ, the normative revelation in the Christian tradition. But in what sense can any single historical person or event be normative?

RELATIVISM AND REVELATION

Relativism is a necessary consequence of the self's relational being:" . . . all knowledge is conditioned by the standpoint of the knower."[1] Niebuhr analyzes this relational standpoint in terms of psychological, historical, and religious relativism.

Three factors result in *psychological relativism*. First, all persons are restricted to a certain range of sensitivity, and particular persons have limitations within that range. None of us is able to hear certain audio frequencies that are heard by other animals, and some of us are unable to hear sounds that are easily heard by most humans. Limited sensitivity, either through the absence of the necessary faculty or through neglect, is also true with respect to the more complicated and subtle combinations of the senses.

A second factor resulting in psychological relativism is the restriction imposed by each individual's perspective. Where and when we stand in space and time makes a difference as to what we are able to experience. I cannot witness a robbery on the other side of town while I am reading in my study. As a customer standing in the bank I do not see the robbery as I would if I were passing in the street as the robbers make their escape. The relational self has its uniqueness, in part, by virtue of its perspective. No one else can fully share my point of view. But my point of view also sets limits on what I am able to experience and know.

Along with the limitations imposed by sensitivity and perspective, there is the limitation imposed by reason. The mental tools we bring to any event restrict what we are able to know of that event. It takes more than acute sense organs and a seat on the fifty-yard line to experience the game of football as football. Without some knowledge of the rules of the game, the scene is simply one of semi-controlled violence.

Niebuhr's recognition of psychological relativism is not a denial of the reality of what is seen and understood under the particular limits of sensitivity, perspective, and reason. The symphony is real even though I only sense some of its movement in harmony and range. A robbery has actually taken place even though I only see the thieves leap into the getaway car. The football team has been penalized fifteen yards even though I do not understand the offensive holding rules. To acknowledge psychological relativism is simply to acknowledge that objects are known under the conditions of the knower's relation to those objects.

Historical relativism is a further specification of psychological relativism. It is entailed by the historical nature of reason itself. If it is the case that objects are known under the conditions of the knower's relation to those objects, and if it is also the case that no self-other relation can be completely abstracted from the self/social companion relation, then social reason is an ingredient in all knowledge. Social reason, like the social self, changes through time. The mental tools employed by the medieval scholastic were not those of the first-century Palestinian Jew, nor are our rational forms just like those of our grandparents. A person's particular place in space-time is also a point in social-cultural history. That particularity affects not only one's vision but the rational equipment one brings to that vision. Historical relativism, as the phrase

is used by Niebuhr, means that the categories of reason themselves, not just their employment, are relative to the standpoint
of the observer:" . . . our reason is not only in space-time but
. . . time-space is in our reason."[2]

Niebuhr discusses reason in terms of categories, concepts,
patterns, images, and symbols we employ in our interpretation
of the entities with which we stand in relation. These rational
tools have a wide range of applicability, and Niebuhr gives them
no precise definition. Basically, however, they function in the
apprehension and expression of our actual situation.

Sometimes an image comprehends and articulates a single,
fairly unified, entity, feeling, or event. The outline of the Empire
State Building represents New York City; a rose may evoke the
sense of love. Sometimes a symbol in its particularity serves as
the interpretive clue for a pattern of meaning that encompasses
numerous entities, feelings, and events over an extended period
of time. The Declaration of Independence, evolution, Auschwitz—such images lend form and intelligibility to experience by
relating particulars to one another in larger wholes that are
themselves meaningful. The tools of reason are patterns of interpretation, images that structure our relational interaction in
meaningful contexts.

Symbolic form is a term Niebuhr employs in describing the
function of reason. A symbolic form is an interpretive image that
simultaneously represents and shapes experience. In Niebuhr's
usage the concept of symbolic form stresses the reciprocity between subject and object, the active role played by both observer and observed in the formation of knowledge. In citing art
as evidence of our symbolic, image-using character, Niebuhr states
that pictorial representation "not only mirrors but guides men's
changing apprehensions of actuality."[3] We have already seen this
dual function of symbolic form in Niebuhr's description of responsibility as a report of experience and an instrument of analysis.

Symbolic forms are not chosen arbitrarily. They are products
of interaction between subject and object, between the experiencing self and the reality experienced. "Actuality always extends beyond the patterns of ideas into which we want to force

it."[4] Some symbolic forms are more adequate than others because they comprehend a greater part of our experience. So it is that Niebuhr prefers responsibility symbolism to that of achievement or duty. Imagery taken from the common experience of persons in responsive dialogue brings into focus aspects of the relational self that other images ignore or obscure. New situations are forever modifying our images as reports of experience. These same images, as instruments of analysis, are continually shaping the understanding of things that informs our response and thereby modifies the situation.

The numerous symbolic forms operative in human understanding constitute one of the three factors that contribute to psychological relativism. But these forms and images are themselves subject to limitation. Were the same set of symbolic forms universally employed, the limits of sensitivity, perspective, and reason would be the sole basis of relativism. But, as Niebuhr puts the matter, "we are required in our time to recognize the further fact that the reason which operates in this restricted field is itself limited by its historical and social character."[5]

Historical relativism refers to the fact that the images and patterns that condition human knowledge are themselves conditioned. They are finite particulars as temporal as the data they organize. To abstract them from the social-cultural milieu in which they originate does not automatically give them universal status.

Historical relativism is a logical consequence of relational selfhood in a network of interaction and change.

> There seems to be no perception of anything which does not contain an interpretation, and there is no interpretation which is not a function of our social communication as well as of our interaction with the objects. Communication is a three-way process in which an active questioning and answering, interpreting and correcting goes on not simply between speaker and hearer but between both of these and their common objects.
>
> Yet further, there are no really common objects except in a society in which the symbolic process goes on. . . . [6]

The social-temporal self is never in precisely the same situation twice, and thus the dialogue between the symbolic forms of reason and the relationships they serve to interpret is continual. Furthermore, the emergence and development of symbolic forms is subject to the joint authorship of the self and its social companions in numerous triadic relationships. Historical relativism, as Niebuhr uses the phrase, involves relations in being as well as in time. It points to the fluidity of images and patterns employed by the self standing in a particular relation to all others in the temporal series of events, to all others in a present social-cultural environment, and to a company of social companions that varies from one situation to the next.

Historical relativism does not deny the reality of what is known; it does take seriously the significance of the relational standpoint of the knower. Looking back on his own use of "historical relativism," Niebuhr suggests that "historical relationism" might be more adequate.[7] The former term implies a subjectivism he does not intend. Relativism points to the partiality of knowledge, not the incompleteness or absence of the known. The relational self can step outside neither the conditions of all human experiences nor the particular social-temporal context in which that experience takes place for it. In acknowledging these consequences of relational selfhood, relativism does not excuse ignorance and error; it does deny the possibility of human omniscience.

In defending his view of historical relativism against agnostic consequences, Niebuhr sometimes uses the term "animal faith" to stand for the acceptance of the reality of what we see in psychologically and historically conditioned experience. Animal faith sustains what Niebuhr calls *objective relativism*. The self is objectively relativistic when it proceeds with "confidence in the independent reality of what is seen, though recognizing that its assertions about that reality are meaningful only to those who look upon it from the same standpoint."[8] One must subject his or her assertions to the criticism of others who have a different perspective as well as those who share the same standpoint. But one need not deny the existence of absolutes nor give up the search for universal truths. Objective relativism recognizes the partiality of human knowledge per se and the particular partiality of individual knowers. It invokes the critical method in order that exclusive perspectives and finite formulations not be mistaken for inclusive wisdom timelessly expounded. The fact that the self always stands in triadic relationships that involve other knowers operates as a natural though not always sufficient check on subjectivism.

Whereas psychological and historical relativism apply to all human knowledge, *religious relativism* applies only to our knowledge of the gods. Niebuhr's strongest statement of religious relativism is that "one can speak and think significantly about God only from the point of view of faith in him."[9] Religious relativism has its basis in Niebuhr's definition of God or the gods as objects of faith, objects of trust and loyalty, thirds in the most important instance of the cause triad. Given such a definition, this form of relativism seems to follow necessarily. If God is the object of faith, how could we know God apart from faith? God, the objective reality, cannot be separated from faith, the subjective activity. Faith is to God as sense experience is to natural entities. Religious relativism, unlike its psychological and historical partners, is not simply pointing to a limited perspective; it is pointing to the only perspective.

As a Protestant theologian, a person "who seeks to understand what he believes with the aid of Protestant theology,"[10] Niebuhr has a religious interest in God. That is to say, he is concerned with the deity value of God, the value a reality has as the satisfaction of the religious need for that which makes life worth living. It is not the human desire for a god or the self's awareness of its religious need that sustains deity value. This value, like all others, is the consequence of an objective relationship between valued and valuing beings. Values are objectively relativistic, though now that phrase refers to the object rather than the mode of inquiry whereby it is accessible. The stubborn independence of reality is exemplified in the conflict and frustration that is engendered by polytheistic and henotheistic forms of faith. The embodiments of these forms go against the grain of the universe.

So it is that Niebuhr can speak of psychological, historical, and religious relativism and at the same time call for *religious realism*.[11] Religious realism has an objective interest and a critical method. While confident in the independent reality of the religious object, it is aware of the ease with which the relative can be mistaken for the absolute. While related to God in faith and with social companions similarly trusting and loyal, the religious realist is aware of the temptation to make that faith or that community its god. The basis of religious realism and objective relativism in Niebuhr's theology is twofold. The self lives and moves and has its being in the One beyond the many, and the self is social and time-full, even in its relation to the One.

The consequence of relativism for revelation is that we cannot think about God except as historical and religious beings. History reveals faith and its objects because history is the medium in which faith expresses itself. The faithful self is social and time-full and cannot stand outside of history. Faith interprets and shapes history. Faith orients our actions and establishes our communities in the present. It gives meaning to past and future. If God is an object of faith known only in and to faith, and if faith is inescapably wedded to history, then the revelation of God will be so wedded. "We are in history as the fish is in water and what we mean by the revelation of God can be indicated only as we point through the medium in which we live."[12]

Niebuhr makes a distinction between *external history*, history as seen, and *internal history*, history as lived. In external history events are regarded from the outside. The nonparticipating observer deals in abstract description and serial or quantitative measurements. The result is a history of things. In internal history events are apprehended from within. Seen by the participant, they are part of a personal or communal destiny. The result is a history of selves.

The difference between external and internal history is the difference between the accounts of a political crisis given by a foreign correspondent and a national patriot, or the accounts of a sunset given by a scientist and a poet. The difference between external and internal history is the difference between the description of a child's illness given by the physician and the mother, or the descriptions of poverty given by a public official and a welfare recipient.

The distinction between external and internal history is a distinction between perspectives. The same event can be subjected to both views, though different aspects of the event will be apparent according to the standpoint from which it is apprehended. Niebuhr's example of contrasting descriptions of the event that brought our nation into being is worth repeating here:

> Lincoln's Gettysburg Address begins with history: "Four-score and seven years ago our fathers brought forth upon this continent a new nation, conceived in liberty and dedicated to the proposition that all men are created free and equal." The same event is described in the *Cambridge Modern History* in the following fashion: "On July 4, 1776, Congress passed the resolution which made the colonies independent communities, issuing at the same time the well-known Declaration of Independence. If we regard the Declaration as the assertion of an abstract political theory, criticism and condemnation are easy. It sets out with a general proposition so vague as to be practically useless. The doctrine of the equality of men, unless it be qualified and conditioned by reference to special circumstance, is either a barren truism or a delusion."[13]

Niebuhr contends that the historian's terms, very different than those of the statesperson in this example, have no monopoly on descriptive adequacy. The question of truth and falsity here does not lie between the two accounts but within each in its own context. In Lincoln's case the judgment rests with his fellow citizens who share the same inner history. The author of the *Cambridge Modern History* account turns to colleagues in the field of social and political history for an evaluation of the description. The exclusive use of either approach leaves out significant aspects of our lives as social selves.

The external-internal distinction in Niebuhr's view of history is a variation of the nature-cause distinction in triadic relations among persons. In the case of internal history, self and social companions are related by a common commitment that focuses their perspective on historical events. "An inner history, life's flow as regarded from the point of view of living selves, is always an affair of faith."[14]

Reason is not to be associated any less with internal than with external history. Reason makes use of symbols and images whether it is functioning in the service of a committed participant or an uncommitted observer. Niebuhr argues that personal, reflective images are most appropriate for reason operating in the context of cause relationships and internal history. "The question which is relevant for the life of the self among selves is not whether personal images should be employed but only what personal images arc right and adequate and which are evil imaginations of the heart."[15] The use of inadequate symbolic forms, like faith in inadequate objects of trust and loyalty, results in frustration and divisiveness.

Revelation is that historical event in the life of the self and its social companions that orients reason in its interpretive task and establishes faith in an object of trust and loyalty. Revelation is an organizing principle and a transforming power.

As an *organizing principle* revelation provides the self with an image through which it can find meaning in all its relations of commitment to causes and social companions, a symbol through which it can grasp and shape its internal history. Revelation, in this sense, is a special instance of symbolic form. The revelatory event is that event in our internal history that makes the rest of our history meaningful. Through this special occasion the reasoning self seeks to discover a pattern of dramatic unity whereby it can come to an understanding of its relational selfhood. Operating as an organizing principle, revelation brings intelligibility to the trusts and loyalties of the self's past, present, and future.

Revelation serves as a principle of unity in a duration. It is a part of life that gives meaning to the whole. Niebuhr understands the development of relational selves and communities as organic. The revelatory moment is a clue to the entire organism. It functions like a classic piece of drama, an illuminating parable, the decisive point in a conversation. Conceptualization is useful in identifying repetitions and uniformities, but it is secondary to the illumination given by the special occasion itself. The organizing principle is often a person, and it is always personal in the reflective manner of thirds in cause triads. Drawn from the very history it makes intelligible, it represents in its own particularity the general pattern.

As a *transforming power* revelation is the moment in which we are given a new faith. Revelation shapes the self's primitive confidence that life is worth living; it is a fundamental reordering of trust and loyalty. The self has need of a transforming power because its faith is always attached to some center of value that influences its interpretation. The disclosure of an organizing principle can only be effective if it is accompanied by a reattachment of faith.

Revelation is the event that contains the self's first certainty. "Revelation means for us that part of our inner history which illuminates the rest of it and which is itself intelligible."[16] The intrinsic intelligibility, the self-evident truth of revelation, generates the reinterpretation of the self's past, present, and future. Revelation as organizing principle requires revelation as transforming power.

The revelatory occasion in a friendship transforms the partners so that they can never again understand their relationship as they had before. The power of the special deed or gesture is seen in the creative or destructive potency of its repetition. An endearing word in one context can be a devastating declaration in another. The kiss of fellowship can become the kiss of betrayal. Likewise, communal events that really do transform a people exhibit their power in the effects of their celebration. On the Fourth of July we can renew our dedication to life and liberty for all persons, or we can heighten our patriotic zeal for national ascendancy.

Revelation as transforming power is the establishment of a new triadic relation of self, social companions, and cause. The revelatory event is an existential encounter with a personal third, and it becomes a source of self-knowledge and evaluation. This is revelation's intrinsic intelligibility. The self is known and valued by an other. The movement from the other to the self and back to the other is a personal relation between a Thou and an I.

The self's confidence that life is worth living is embodied in a new triad of faith.

The self that is transformed in revelation interprets its relations in light of its new faith. Revelation as a transforming power passes directly to its function as an organizing principle; "something has happened which compels our faith and which requires us to seek rationality and unity in the whole of our history."[17]

SON OF GOD

Niebuhr defines the Christian as one who is a follower of Jesus Christ or a member of that community of persons for whom Jesus Christ is of supreme importance. If we look at these followers and their communities over the past two thousand years, we discover that the descriptions of their leader are many and varied. Niebuhr finds a unity in these descriptions, asserting that all the many followers in their differing communities share an acceptance of one Jesus Christ as their authority. Niebuhr grounds this fundamental unity, as well as his own description of Jesus Christ, in the New Testament: "the Christ who exercises authority over Christians or whom Christians accept as authority is the Jesus Christ of the New Testament; . . . this is a person with definite teachings, a definite character, and a definite fate."[18]

There always have been and there will continue to be debates about the accuracy of the New Testament documents, whether or not Jesus of Nazareth really lived, and what was the self-understanding of this person. But such debates are secondary to the actual presence of Jesus Christ in the Christian's inner history. It is the presence of a person, an active intelligence and will, as opposed to a list of propositions or a conceptual statement. It is simply the case for Niebuhr and his companions that this Jesus Christ of the New Testament has shaped their past, informs their present, and anticipates their future: "I believe that my way of thinking about life, myself, my human companions and our destiny has been so modified by his presence in our history that I cannot get away from his influence."[19]

In his own most extensive effort at a description of Jesus Christ,

Niebuhr chooses the perspective of a moralist. He focuses on the virtues that Christ exemplifies and enjoins upon his followers. For Niebuhr each of these virtues exhibits a fundamental relationship that unites it with all of the others and accounts for the extraordinary practice of each. "The unity of this person lies in the simplicity and completeness of his direction toward God."[20]

Love is often cited as the clue to Jesus' message and the cornerstone of his ethics. Niebuhr affirms the importance of love in any adequate description of Jesus Christ but finds its primary significance as a descriptive virtue in its expression of Jesus' relation to God.

The extreme nature of Jesus' love is "the extremism of devotion to the one God, uncompromised by love of any other absolute good."[21] There is no other object worthy of such devotion, but there are other ways of relating to that object in addition to love. Love does not exhaust the relationship; it has to be understood alongside the other virtues. For Jesus God may be love, but love is not God.

What is most significant about Jesus' love is its object: the Lord of heaven and earth, the transcendent power that creates and destroys, the last reality before which all the objects of all our loves pass. The God whom Jesus loves is "the power who causes rain and sun, without whose will and knowledge not a sparrow dies, nor a city is destroyed, nor he himself crucified."[22] The name "Father" on Jesus' lips is heroic because it is given to the One on whom all women and men are absolutely dependent, the One whom men and women try to deny, or ignore, or appease. The greatness of Jesus' love is its object, which to most of us is anything but fatherlike. If we simply equate God and love, we fail to see the significance of Jesus' love. Jesus' love is an awesome virtue because it characterizes his relation to the One who is slayer as well as life-giver.

In light of this love of God, how are we to understand Jesus' love of neighbor? What is the relation between the two great commandments, to love God *and* neighbor? Only God is to be loved "with all your heart, and with all your soul, and with all your mind, and with all your strength" (Mark 12:30). This is precisely the monotheistic concentration we have noted in Jesus' love. The neighbor is not to be the object of a love of such single-minded intensity. Rather, the neighbor is an object of love on a par with ourselves and all other creatures. The neighbor has his or her worth in relation to the Creator, and this is the basis of the command to "love your neighbor as yourself" (Mark 12:31). The two commandments must be held together because finite relations of love have their ultimate orientation in relation to God.

It is Jesus' complete and unswerving love for God that motivates his love for men and women, but the two loves in question are not identical. Niebuhr refers to the words attributed to Jesus in John 15:12, "Love one another as I have loved you," as a significant reformulation of the Jewish command, "Love thy neighbor as thyself."[23] There is a difference between Jesus' love for God, the center of value, and for women and men, beings valuable in relation to that center. The love for God is marked by adoration, gratitude, and joy, while the love for men and women is pitying, forgiving, and suffering. The former is passion; the latter is compassion. Jesus loves us not as we love each other but as God loves us. Jesus loves us only as a Son of God can love, that is, out of a fundamental and all-pervading love of God. "Because he loves the Father with the perfection of human *eros*, therefore he loves men with the perfection of divine *agape*, since God is *agape*."[24]

Niebuhr claims that Jesus' love for God and his love for neighbor are two distinct virtues that have a common source rather than a common quality. In his devotion to the Creator, Jesus is moved to concern for the creation. And because he loves the transcendent reality, he is not threatened by the passing of finite realities, even his own. Sometimes Jesus' love of God is expressed in anger as when he clears the temple of money-changers. More often it is seen in his love of the unlovable, that is the unlovable according to criteria employed by the dominant culture. Jesus' love for prostitutes and tax collectors is a function of his love for God. Because he loves God as men and women should love God, he is able to love men and women as only God can love. "There seems then to be no other adequate way to describe

Jesus as having the virtue of love than to say that his love was that of the Son of God. It was not love but God that filled his soul."[25]

Given the eschatological imagery of the New Testament, *hope* is sometimes singled out as the key to Jesus' life. The teachings attributed to Jesus suggest the imminent fulfillment of messianic promises. The intense anticipation and eager expectation of divine goodness and justice give an urgency to all that Jesus commands. Some commentators have suggested that these commands are invalidated because the reversal of history did not come. Perhaps Jesus was teaching an interim ethic that has lost its urgency because the interim has lasted two thousand years.

Niebuhr contends that the urgency of Jesus' hope does not derive from a cosmic catastrophe yet to come; rather it is the urgency of a hope in the sustaining power whose universal rulership is now. Jesus' hope was in God, not a particular view of history. "Repent, for the kingdom of heaven is at hand" (Matt. 4:17).

Niebuhr points out that the realization of the present rule of God in the natural and daily course of events is the clue to many of Jesus' most radical ethical statements, statements on which the anticipation of a coming kingdom seems to have little bearing. Take, for example, the admonition to love one's enemies in which Jesus refers to the heavenly Father who "makes his sun rise on the evil and on the good, and sends rain on the just and on the unjust" (Matt. 5:45). Likewise it is to God's feeding of the birds of the air and clothing of the lilies of the field that Jesus refers in his teaching about not being anxious (Matt. 6:25–34). Thus, with hope as with love, it is Jesus' relation to God that explains the extremity of his virtue. The "heroic character of Jesus' hopefulness" has its source in his relation to "the God who is Now as well as Then." Niebuhr asserts, "not eschatology but sonship to God is the key to Jesus' ethics."[26]

Another virtue that has little meaning if abstracted from relations is *faith*. In Jesus' case the faith relation is with God, and we will be misled if we concentrate on faith itself as definitive. We must be very clear about its object. If we look at Jesus for an illustration of faith in one's contemporaries, we discover a real skeptic. Jesus sees his generation as evil and adulterous; he has little confidence even in his own disciples. They are often offended by him; they misunderstand him; and the strongest of them all is not able to stand fast in the time of trial.

Jesus' faith is startling, not because it is faith, but because it is attached to the One of whom we are most suspicious, the One who undermines all our little faiths. Insofar as Jesus is able to bring out goodness in human beings it is by virtue of his faith in God and their relation to God. His reliance on God for everything from his daily bread to the direction of his ministry is awesome next to our dependence on insurance companies and I.Q. tests. Jesus' faith in the Lord of heaven and earth, not his own power of positive thinking, sustained him on the night when all those around him had fled. His is the faith of a Son of God, "too extreme for those who conceive themselves as sons of nature, or of men, or of blind chance."[27]

Some Christian existentialists have taken Jesus' *obedience* as the preeminent virtue. Jesus stands directly and fully before God. His obedient acts seem to transcend the law itself; his very thoughts and motives are set out for judgment. Even at Gethsemane where he wrestles with God over his own destiny, there seems to be little doubt that he will be obedient, even unto death. But Niebuhr contends that this virtue of obedience is as empty as it is radical until we attend to the One to whom Jesus is obedient.

The God Jesus obeys is not a regulative idea or a conceptual counterpart of human decision. It is the Creator and Governor of nature and history. God's will is made known in the Ten Commandments. This One requires that we love the neighbor and that we be merciful. As with love, hope, and faith, the virtue in question is of little significance apart from the relation it describes. Jesus' obedience is radical because it is obedience to the One who transcends all authorities, all principalities and powers. But this One is not simply the Unconditioned met only in a moment of decision. This One is the God whose will is the pattern of existence. The imperative God places on us is one of content as well as form. *What* Jesus decided to do is not to be overlooked in coming to an understanding of his obedience. "It is the obedience of a Son whose sonship is not definable as just obedience to a principle that constrains obedience."[28]

Evident in Jesus' practice of *humility* is the significance of the relation it characterizes. Jesus' humility is before God, not men and women. Were this not the case, his humility would be ambiguous and liable to misunderstanding as a feeling of inferiority or an effort at accommodation. Jesus lives with sinners and outcasts. He accepts indignity and insult. He washes the feet of his disciples. But this same Jesus speaks before the political and religious authorities with confidence. There is neither insecurity nor self-abnegation here. Apology and deference are not Jesus' style. His repudiation of the title "Good Teacher" is not a courtesy to human mores but a statement about his and everyone else's place before God, who alone is good (Luke 18:18–19).

Jesus' humility is not condescension toward the outcast but a selfless freedom that enables him to restore a sense of dignity and worth in those who have been humiliated by the self-declared righteous. Nor is Jesus' humility a form of moderation, an attempt to keep his place on the scale of being. It is by keeping his relation to God foremost that he can be meek and gentle; "the humility of Jesus is humility before God, and can only be understood as the humility of the Son."[29]

For Niebuhr, then, from his own perspective as a moralist developing a description of Jesus Christ in the New Testament, the virtues appear to have their source and mutual integrity in Jesus' relation to God. Whether Jesus' virtues are taken separately or together,

> . . . the strangeness, the heroic stature, the extremism and sublimity of this person, considered morally, is due to that unique devotion to God and to that single-hearted trust in Him which can be symbolized by no other figure of speech so well as by the one which calls him Son of God.[30]

We cannot consider Jesus' moral conduct and teaching without considering the One to whom Jesus is related in all of his acts and sayings. We cannot know the Son without acknowledging the One he continually identifies as Father.

But, according to Niebuhr's analysis, this is only half the moral picture of Jesus Christ in the New Testament. A moral relation to the Creator is necessarily a moral relation to the creation. The Son cannot love his Father without loving his Father's children. And so Jesus' love of God, his perfect human *eros*, is also love of neighbor, perfect divine *agape*. This double movement from person to God and God to person is the basic rhythm Niebuhr finds in the New Testament portraits of Jesus Christ. It is the rhythm of Jesus' moral integrity as he stands at once in relation to God and persons. "In his moral sonship to God Jesus Christ is not a median figure, half God, half man; he is a single person wholly directed as man toward God and wholly directed in his unity with the Father toward men. He is mediatorial, not median."[31] Just as the commandments to love God and neighbor must be held together, so too must Jesus' human *eros* and divine *agape* be understood together. Jesus' love for his neighbor, his selfless teaching and healing, mediates God's love for the creation. Jesus exists as "the focusing point in the continuous alternation of movements from God to man and man to God."[32]

Niebuhr's preference for the Son of God figure of speech derives from his own attempts to describe Jesus Christ in the New Testament. This relational image emerges from and makes sense out of the conduct and teaching of Jesus. It gives Niebuhr a way of speaking at once about Jesus' incredible devotion to God and his utterly uninhibited service of humanity. It symbolizes the substantial relation from which terms such as double movement and mediation are abstracted. The Son of God is a figure that suggests the compelling authority of the New Testament portraits themselves. The presence of Jesus Christ in the Christian's inner history is not simply the memory of a great man. It is the contemporary challenge of a living God.

> The power and attraction Jesus Christ exercises over men never comes from him alone, but from him as Son of the Father. It comes from him in his Sonship in a double way, as man living to God and God living with him. Belief in him and loyalty to his

cause involves men in the double movement from world to God
and from God to world.[33]

The Son of God imagery symbolizes the same relational form
as Niebuhr's triad of faith in which self and social companions are
related in terms of a third, an object of trust and loyalty. This
third is the reference point in a dynamic set of mutual relations
among I's and Thou's. The third is personified in a representative
Thou, a figure who stands for the community of trust and loyalty
while at the same time pointing beyond it. As mediator in the
double movement from selves to God and God to selves, Jesus
Christ is the representative Thou in a preeminent triad of faith:
"You and I and our Neighbor, Jesus Christ, and God, the Father. . . . Here the structure of faith which appears in all our
relationships, it seems to me, appears, in a kind of cosmic form."[34]

Likewise, as the incarnation of radically monotheistic faith,
Jesus Christ gives content to responsibility theory. Response, interpretation, accountability, and social solidarity take on meaning. Jesus is in continual dialogue with the last reality before
which all persons stand. Instead of trying to escape it or pretend
that the encounter comes only in the future, Jesus responds to
the final reality in every present. He responds to it as trustworthy. He calls this One in which the many have their being "Father." "If then we try to summarize the ethos of Jesus in a formula
we may do so by saying that he interprets all actions upon him
as signs of the divine action of creation, government, and salvation and so responds to them as to respond to divine action."[35]
In Jesus Christ the responsive self is given the answer to the
question, "To whom am I responding and in what community of
interaction?"

The vitality of the New Testament does not rest in its exhibition of a triadic faith structure or a double movement mediated
by a self-transcending third. Nor is its primary appeal in the ex-
emplification of responsibility theory. The New Testament has its
power in the figure of Jesus Christ as Son of God, as one who
draws us into present relations with God and other persons. For
this reason Niebuhr urges men and women to return again and

again to the Scriptures. There, in the company of their social companions, they will encounter the Son of God, the person Jesus, who is called the Christ because he is a mediator, one so related to God that he relates others to God.

SYMBOLIC FORM

We recall that for Niebuhr a symbolic form is an interpretive image that simultaneously mirrors and shapes experience. As a concept, symbolic form describes the representative and formative function of reason in the midst of relational selfhood, in the midst of the reciprocity between knower and known. Niebuhr's understanding of revelation and history turns on the function of particular historic occasions as symbolic forms, interpretive images that elucidate entire histories.

As the special occasion that illumines and directs the Christian's life, Jesus Christ functions as a symbolic form:

> . . . in Christian life Jesus Christ is a symbolic form with the aid of which men tell each other what life and death, God and man, are *like*; but even more he is a form which they employ as an a priori, an image, a scheme or pattern in the mind which gives form and meaning to their experience.[36]

Jesus Christ exhibits the same duality we have noted in other interpretive images. He is a symbol of the way things are, a mirror of one's actual experience, and he is a guide in one's own activity. He is a factor in the understanding and the shaping of the self's relations.

The figure of Jesus Christ, his teachings, and the events associated with his life, death, and resurrection serve as provocative parables in the dialogical relation of knower and known. The birth narratives with their mixture of shepherds and kings, stars and stables, beckon men and women to seek God's presence in the midst of life's variety and uncertainty. Persons for whom Jesus Christ is a symbolic form cannot neglect nature's manifold signs. Jesus teaches his followers to consider how grass grows in the fields, how seeds burst into new life that flourishes or fades.

The one for whom Jesus Christ is a symbolic form cannot

neglect the manifold signs in all that is alien. The Gospel accounts deal with prostitutes, tax collectors, soldiers, poor and diseased men and women. Their presence in the New Testament is not an argument that they should be granted the social status of scribes and Pharisees; they are present because they understand what scribes and Pharisees can neither hear nor see.

The magnetism of this symbolic form, the Jesus Christ of the New Testament, is due to its ambiguity, its unwillingness to yield to our preconceptions. It is a personal figure continually urging us beyond our present definitions, pointing out new life where we have failed to look. The personal mystery of Jesus Christ as interpretive image keeps us continually off balance.

Jesus Christ as symbolic form evokes identification. A memory of two thousand years becomes a reality now when a stranger moves into our neighborhood, when the hungry ask us to share our bread, when the political prisoner seeks our support. Understood through Jesus Christ as symbolic form, the needy companion is "a Christo-morphic being, apprehended as in the form of Christ, something like Christ, though another."[37]

Jesus Christ as symbolic form evokes imitation. Some of us have worked very hard at being Christ-like. Sometimes the effort is to adopt Jesus' style. We try to follow his teachings, or copy his conduct, or love as he loved. Sometimes the imitation becomes an attempt to have Jesus take over our lives in a controlling way, making our decisions for us. But whether we want to follow in Christ's footsteps or have him actually take those footsteps for us, we discover again the mystery of this person. Jesus is at once attractive and disconcerting because in getting to know him we come to know much more than him. We are drawn to this figure like the disciples, and like the disciples we discover more than we bargained for.

Jesus Christ points beyond himself. As symbolic form he draws us into encounter with the One before whom we are unique selves. The same Jesus who refuses the title "Good Teacher" lays bare the particular disobedience of one who has observed all the laws from his youth (Luke 18:18–24). A surprising feature of this symbolic form is that in the effort to appropriate it as a model, we discover ourselves in a new context. The one whom we had hoped might relieve us of responsibility brings us face to face with the God of universal responsibility.

In the conjunction of the symbolic forms of Jesus Christ and responsiveness, the Christian is given an *organizing principle* for self-understanding and guidance. In Jesus Christ the Christian has a demonstration of universal responsibility. But this demonstration is also the reconciliation of selves to God. As the incarnation of radically monotheistic faith, Jesus Christ is the disclosure of God's faithfulness. As the representative Thou in the faith triad that includes God and persons, Jesus Christ mediates God's concern for humanity. In his own trust and loyalty he reflects the One who is worthy of such complete commitment. What was for Jesus a response to God becomes for his successors a revelation of God. The event that elicits faith as confidence and loyalty is a demonstration of loyalty and the disclosure of a cause. The Jesus in whom faith was elicited himself becomes the elicitor, the Christ, the *transforming power*.

> On the one hand he appears as the perfect illustration or the incarnate pattern, as the first and only Christian. On the other hand his personal, historical action is understood as God's way of making what is impossible for men possible. . . . Thus he is understood as man, perfectly directed toward God as his end, or perfectly obedient to the Father; and he is acknowledged as divine, as the power of God or as act or Word of God that redirects men who had lost their relation to their end, become enslaved to false goals or had fallen into disobedience. . . . Christ always has something of this double character. In him man is directed toward God; in him also God is directed toward men.[38]

It is more difficult to describe the divinity of Jesus Christ, the sense in which he is the power of God, than it is to describe his demonstration of responsible selfhood. Yet it is the divine empowerment manifest in the Son of God that is fundamental in Niebuhr's understanding of revelation. He contends that the heart of revelation is on the order of the I-Thou, self/social companion relation. A self can be known only on its own initiative. Another self that receives and responds to that disclosure undergoes a change. This is the basis of self-knowledge on an interpersonal level. For Niebuhr, then, the question of revelation is what person it is "who reveals himself in our history in such fashion that we gain a certainty which forces us to seek an intelligible unity in all our life as selves."[39]

Niebuhr rejects the answer that this person is Jesus. Certainly Jesus is a worthy person to follow, and in his life and death one is confronted with valuable insights into the character of the twentieth century as well as the first. But one is also taken beyond this person. As we have seen again and again in Niebuhr's descriptions, it is the mediating character of the New Testament figure that is revelatory. Jesus Christ is the representative Thou in a triad of faith.

> When we say revelation we point to something in the historical event more fundamental and more certain than Jesus. . . . Revelation means God, God who discloses himself to us through our history as our knower, our author, our judge and our only savior.[40]

In revelation we "know ourselves to be known from beginning to end." Unlike all the others who know us partially, this One knows us fully and so is the source of a new kind of knowledge about ourselves. In revelation the author of this history that seemed to be without purpose or plot greets us. "We are surprised by the knowledge of someone there in the darkness and the void of human life." In revelation all our narrow judgments are upset, not by the equally narrow judgments of our friends and enemies, but by the One before whom all heads are bowed. In revelation all our saviors, our tanks and our tinsel, our high rises and our high ideals, our pot and our politics, are put to shame by the One who has already saved us. "When the unfairness of all the fair prices we have placed on things is shown up; when the great riches of God reduce our wealth to poverty, that is revelation."[41]

The meaning of revelation as divine self-disclosure can only be expressed in personal acts of response. Niebuhr not only admits this, he asserts it as part of any description of revelation. The self-disclosure of the infinite person can only be acknowledged in personal confession: you are my God.

Once one recognizes that the heart of Christian revelation is a personal encounter with God and that its certainty can only be confessed, what more can be said? Niebuhr is fully aware of the difficulties this question poses for the theologian. These difficulties can never be surmounted if one is looking for logical arguments or metaphysical proofs. But there are ways of approaching the problem of revelation as personal encounter. One such way is to describe what happens to the self.

We have seen that the self is absolutely dependent on the radical action whereby it has its being and has it in a particular time and place. The last reality at the limits of the self's social-temporal existence is also the end of the movement through causes that point beyond themselves. The universal intent characterizing that movement seems finally to come to nothing. Faced with this abyss, the self returns to its objects of trust and loyalty, its gods. Sometimes these are closed societies, nations or institutions or social-political movements that sustain the self's confidence and enlist its support for relatively long periods. Sometimes the gods are particular self-interests, pleasures, persons, or goals that are held simultaneously or in rapid succession. Whether the form of faith be henotheistic or polytheistic, it is always socially or internally divisive. What is more disconcerting is that our gods lead us to the very abyss we sought to escape. Social movements, like men and women, are born to make their contribution and then make way for others. Nations, like flowers, flourish and then fade. Pleasures, whether of the mind or of the body, are destined to dust and decay if they do not lead to boredom sooner. However grand such finite entities and entertainments may be on a limited scale, they are failures as objects of trust and loyalty on a universal scale.

> The tragedy of our religious life is not only that it divides us within ourselves and from each other. There is a greater tragedy—the twilight of the gods. None of these beings on which we rely to give content and meaning to our lives is able to supply continuous meaning and value. The causes for which we live all die.[42]

When we try to account for the twilight of our gods, we discover the same reality that stands at the limits of our social-
temporal selfhood. The radical action that thrusts us into existence and then removes us is also responsible for the rise and fall
of all our gods. What might have remained a neutral void becomes an enemy. Whether we call it the nature of things, or fate,
or the last reality, it surrounds our life. "What it is we do not
know save that it is and that it is the supreme reality with which
we must reckon."[43] Only if this supreme reality were somehow
to become the object of our trust and loyalty, could we satisfy our
faith that life is worth living. Only if we could be reconciled to
this slayer of all that is dear to us, could we stop making our
frustrating and divisive retreats into polytheism and henotheism.
It is just this reconciliation that Niebuhr claims takes place in
revelation.

> Now a strange thing has happened in our history and in our
> personal life; our faith has been attached to that great void, to
> that enemy of all our causes, to that opponent of all our gods.
> The strange thing has happened that we have been enabled to
> say of this reality, this last power in which we live and move and
> have our being, "Though it slay us yet will we trust it."[44]

In revelation as transforming power the self is reconciled to
the One beyond the many, the One on whom the many and the
self are absolutely dependent. The last reality becomes the object of trust and loyalty, the center of value and the cause. The
faith that was misdirected to the gods of henotheism and polytheism is attached to being itself. In the power of revelation
the self is transformed. Using a phrase Niebuhr quotes from
Alfred North Whitehead, this is the "transition from God the
void to God the enemy, and from God the enemy to God the
companion."[45]

That such a transition has taken place in communal and personal histories, Niebuhr finds undeniable. Furthermore, for
Niebuhr himself, the transforming reconciliation of God and persons always takes place in association with Jesus Christ.

> I do not have the evidence which allows me to say that the mir-
> acle of faith in God is worked only by Jesus Christ and that it is

never given to men outside the sphere of his working, though I may say that where I note its presence I posit the presence also of something like Jesus Christ.[46]

Jesus Christ accomplishes a "strange miracle" in relational selves. "He turns their reasoning around so that . . . the *Gestalt* which they bring to their experiences of suffering as well as of joy, of death as well as of life, is the *Gestalt*, the symbolic form, of grace."[47] The transformation that Jesus Christ empowers is never fully accomplished in the life of a self. The attachment of faith to the Determiner of Destiny is not total and continuous. Yet the hope for complete reconciliation and a life of responsibility in universal community is partially fulfilled. The potential for transformation has been and will continue to be realized fragmentarily.

Perhaps the most difficult question to ask of revelation as personal encounter with God is how such transforming reconciliation could take place through Jesus Christ. "How Jesus Christ in history, and the symbolic Christ within, reconciles men to God, or God to men, or accomplishes the double reconciliation of each to each, Christians cannot easily say."[48] It is strange that the earthly fate of the one whom Niebuhr calls the incarnation of radical faith does not confirm the self's suspicion of the Determiner of Destiny. Everywhere Jesus turns during the final days of his life, he is cruelly betrayed. All his followers, only a short while ago loudly proclaiming their commitment, are now rapidly retreating. First they are unable to watch with Jesus at Gethsemane. Then they panic and flee, the strongest of them positively denying any association with the man from Galilee.

The New Testament narratives of the trial before the Sanhedrin and the procurator are among the most powerful literary depictions of human aloneness. Apparently there was not even that dedicated handful we have seen standing trial so often in our own time. The passion story is not about the Jerusalem Thirteen, it is about the Jerusalem One. A single word could have reunited Jesus with his friends. Apparently the word that Pilate wanted would not have been a fitting response to God. And so he went to be hung on a cross, this radically faithful, responsible self.

How can this possibly be the event that elicits our trust in the last reality? Jesus echoes our own cry of despair before the One who destroys all our dreams: "My God, my God, why hast thou forsaken me?" (Mark 15:34). Certainly at Golgotha we meet God the enemy.

The miracle with which Niebuhr struggles is a present one. "How is faith in God possible?" How does Jesus Christ as symbolic form work the contemporary transformation from God the enemy to God the companion? Niebuhr's assertion is not that there was a single miraculous intervention of God two thousand years ago. Niebuhr's assertion is that the spirit of the slain Jesus is unconquerable. This is the resurrection, that the one who was faithful even unto death is a present transforming power. The transition from God the enemy to God the friend is inseparably connected with the man whose response of trust and loyalty was answered in resurrection from the dead. "Of that resurrection we may know no more than that he lives and is powerful over us and among us."[49]

For Niebuhr the resurrection, whatever else it may be, is the victory of universal trust over suspicion, of universal loyalty over disloyalty. This victory is won whenever and wherever selves are reconciled to God. The establishment of friendship between God and persons is, for Niebuhr, the key problem in human existence. It is in terms of this problem that Niebuhr understands Jesus Christ as revelation, as that transforming power working in our midst to the end that we may respond to the One beyond the many as Friend.

CHAPTER III

God

The primary consequence of revelation is a revolution in our relation to God. What was present but hidden behind the distorted forms of misplaced trust and the hazy reflections of distracting loyalties is revealed. Revelation, as Niebuhr understands it, is not a cataclysmic alteration in the structures of being; it is a revolutionary movement within a dynamic relationship.

In Jesus Christ the recurring points of tension in Niebuhr's analysis of selfhood become sources of creative energy. The basic human confidence that life is worth living is fulfilled in a worthy attachment, one that opens up rather than restricts the self. Integrity is found in response to a universal other in which all particulars participate; the final reality is encountered as friend rather than foe. All this happens in a process aptly described as reconciliation. God is revealed in Jesus Christ, a symbolic form that provides at once an adequate interpretation of human existence and the empowerment to act on that interpretation.

What can be said of God on the basis of the divine disclosure reflects the twofold nature of revelation as organizing principle and transforming power. This distinction, made in the interest of clarity, should not qualify our understanding of revelation as an event in which interpretation and enabling power are intimately related, an event in which we encounter the One in and beyond the many as First Person.

THE ONE IN AND BEYOND THE MANY

The God revealed in Jesus Christ is the One in and beyond the many. God's rule is manifest in nature and history. The Lord of heaven and earth is present in the glory of a Sierra sunrise and the squalor of a Newark tenement. Divine sovereignty is exercised in everything that happens. Jesus does not direct our attention to an idea of God; he points to the reality of God in the world. There are no realms from which the activity of God is excluded. We are as close to this One in politics as in religion. We are under the reign of this One in our deeds as well as our thoughts. This is the radical force of the word "One." There is no other present in all that we do and have done to us. The single identity in all of life and death, star and stone, love and hate is this One, this Creator-sustainer-destroyer of all that was and is and ever shall be.

It is this One in and beyond the many that Niebuhr speaks of as the principle of being. He purposely identifies the God revealed in Jesus Christ as the "principle" of being rather than the "highest" or "most powerful" being. God is not *a* being. God is beyond being as the One in whom all existents live and move and have their being. God is the One beyond the many in whom the many participate and in whom the many are related. God is the One on whom the self is absolutely dependent for its beginning, sustenance, and end in being.

This is but half the description of God that follows from divine self-disclosure in Jesus Christ. This universal singularity can also be trusted. The Creator of flowers, the sustainer of nations, the destroyer of loved ones is good.

So it is also this One in and beyond the many that Niebuhr speaks of as the principle of value. God is not the highest or the supreme value. God is not *a* value, but rather the One beyond value to which all values are finally related. God is the One beyond the many in whom the many participate and in whom the many are related in value as well as in being. Life is worth living because it is lived in relation to God.

In Jesus Christ the Lord of heaven and earth is revealed as a ruler of love.

> What gives the ethical teaching of Jesus its special character is not simply the strength of the conviction that God's rule will

be made wholly manifest; it is even more his certainty that God
who rules nature and history is holy love.[1]

This is the great reconciliation. In abstract terms it is the identification of the principle of being and the principle of value. It is
the revelation that the One in and beyond the many, the final
reality, is God, which is to say "good."

In terms of radical monotheism, revelation is God's self-
disclosure as the universal center of value and the universal cause.
God alone is the adequate object of trust and loyalty, for in God
all being and all value are ultimately united. God is the objective
counterpart of radically monotheistic faith, faith that "dethrones
all absolutes short of the principle of being itself" while it "reverences every relative existent."[2]

Seen in these terms, Jesus Christ is the incarnation of radically monotheistic faith. His confidence in the Creator freed him
to act without fear on behalf of all creation. Because nothing in-
terrupted his relation to God, nothing distorted his relations among
women and men. He saw the real needs of body and mind and
was able to heal what really needed to be made whole and teach
what really needed to be known; he was a person who "single-
mindedly accepted the assurance that the Lord of heaven and
earth was wholly faithful to him and to all creatures, and who in
response gave wholehearted loyalty to the realm of being."[3]

The identity of being and value in the One in and beyond the
many orients our faith that life is worth living. The only object
worthy of our ultimate trust, the only object that has deity value,
is the One we meet in the twilight of all our finite gods, those
objects in which we place our trust only to be betrayed. The
revealed God frees the self from the frustration and fear that
prevail as long as God is hidden. This revelation is a revolution
because the finite gods themselves are liberated. Family and vocation, nation and political program, natural beauty and pleasure
no longer need to bear the burden of our faith that all of life is
worth living. Now these gods can fulfill themselves in relation to
one another and in relation to the One beyond the many. All
beings are open to exploration; all relative goods are praisewor-

thy. Knowing the truth and doing the good are not automatic consequences of revelation; they are real possibilities rooted in the friendship of God and persons. When the One in and beyond the many appears as the power of being and the value of relation, the self is engaged in a continuous revolution of mind and heart.

As the One in and beyond the many, God brings into focus the struggle for self-integrity. The complex relational interaction that characterizes human existence has its unity in God. All parties to the interaction are fundamentally related to the principle of being and value. Though the self responds in a multiplicity of relations, it is always responding to God. The unity of the self in all its roles reflects the final unity of all the patterns of constancy in which those roles are appropriate. When the self confronts the power behind the radical act whereby it *is* itself, it confronts the power whereby all beings *are* in their particularity. The self is one in all its responses to finite action because all those responses are to the One action. "In religious language, the soul' and God belong together; or otherwise stated, I am one within myself as I encounter the One in all that acts upon me."[4]

Revelation speaks to social as well as internal divisiveness. The individual acts to which the self responds are interpreted in a context of relations. If the self is responding to the action of the One in and beyond the many, it must make its interpretation in a context of relations that is universal in extent. To respond to the principle of being and value is to respond within the universal realm of being in which whatever is, is good. "When I respond to the One creative power, I place my companions, human and subhuman and superhuman, in the one universal society which has its center neither in me nor in any finite cause but in the Transcendent One."[5] International as well as interpersonal conflict is the distortion of a fundamental unity in being and value.

The problem of personal identity and integrity of action in complex relational selfhood is not simply a matter of subjective interpretation. The One *beyond* the many is objectively present *in* the many. The intention and rule of God is actual, though often hidden. This hiddenness is not divine perversity. It follows from the fact that God is the One in and beyond the many rather

than one of the many. What perversity there is in God's hiddenness is the result of distorted human interpretations born of distrust
and suspicion.

The revolutionary character of the transition from God hidden to God revealed is most evident with respect to the problem
of contingency. When the self acknowledges that life has its
meaning and value in relation to the One in and beyond the
many, it is accepting the last reality on which it is absolutely
dependent as trustworthy and loyal. Certainly such an acceptance cannot be solely the result of an organizing principle. Though
the Christ-event may illumine and even resolve many of the tensions and ambiguities of relational selfhood, something else must
happen if we are to turn in trust and loyalty to "that last being
which crowns with destruction the life which proceeds from it."[6]
Such a turning must be less like discovering a principle than
being met by a person.

FIRST PERSON

The God revealed in Jesus Christ is the One in and beyond
the many encountered as First Person. The One in question here
is not a concept of the constitution of the universe but an infi-
nitely active deity. In responding to revelation, the self is
responding to "the presence of one faithful person in the multiplicity of the events that happen to the self."[7] Faith as trust and
loyalty is elicited by the revelation of being as faithful. Integrated selfhood is not so much the result of an interpretive scheme
that focuses on the One in and beyond the many, as it is the self's
acknowledgment that its ultimate environment is a trustworthy
Thou. "This God who is the ground of man's whole life is a personal God of complete integrity."[8]

The self-disclosure of God as First Person, the demonstration
of the One in and beyond the many as personal integrity, is the
fundamental assurance on which the self's interpretations are
based. "In dealing with revelation we refer to something in our
history to which we always return as containing our first certainty."[9] Self-knowledge is rooted in reflective personal relations;
in knowing other Thous we come to know ourselves. This is em-

inently so in the self-disclosure of God. It is the revelation of the ultimate Thou that transforms the self.

Talk about the identity of the principle of being and the principle of value is helpful when we are dealing with the revelatory event as an organizing principle that guides the employment of responsibility symbolism. Talk about the First Person is more appropriate when we are dealing with the revelatory event as the great reconciliation that empowers responsible selfhood. Revelation in this sense is God herself or God himself. As transforming power, revelation is God's self-demonstration as my author, my knower, my judge, and my savior. In revelation I am met by the One who sustains me in all my relations and who knows how ambiguous are my claims and commitments in those relations. In revelation I am met by the One whose judgment is beyond excuse because this One considers even my deepest secrets. In revelation I am met by the One who values me and all the entities to which I am related, thereby transvaluating all my own evaluations.

It is *appropriate* to use first person pronouns in referring to the recipient of revelation. The acknowledgment that the ultimate power is personal is itself highly personal. "The immediacy of the self's relation to the power by which it is cannot be supplanted by the mediation of any group of believers. . . . faith as trust and distrust is inexpugnably personal."[10] This does not deny that the self is social in its relation to God, nor does it preclude social corroboration of the self's immediate intuition. Rather it affirms the primitive nature of the God-person relationship.

A personal relation to God defines the character of social selfhood and the extent of responsible selfhood. Faith in God, the First Person, qualifies all the self's relations and holds the self accountable in all those relations. All action takes place in the presence of the one God who is not an idea in our minds, but the reality that confronts and challenges us in all nature and all history. The triadic structure entailed by faith relationship with God includes the entire realm of being. Universal responsibility takes place in a universal triad of faith. Niebuhr speaks of the ethics of Jesus as the ethics of "a single community, the community of which God, the Father, is author and ruler and in which relations to him are always of decisive importance."[11] These relations cannot be severed from the self's relations in nature and society, and so the reconciliation of God and the self is the first part of a double movement that is only completed in the reconciliation of God and the world.

The transforming power of revelation is the power of universal reconciliation. This is the revolutionary character of Jesus Christ, that he is the decisive turning point in the relation of men and women to the First Person and thus to all persons. Through Jesus Christ one's fundamental relation is transformed and with that begins the transformation of all one's relations; the self-disclosure of the First Person initiates and sustains a permanent revolution. This revolution includes the radical reconstruction of our sense of unity, power, and goodness.

A common solution to the problem of *unity* in the self and in its environment is to posit a single unconditioned being beyond the multitude of conditioned beings. But the God revealed in Jesus Christ is the One *in* as well as beyond the many. This One is not a distant observer but a present conditioner. God's unity and the unity God intends for the world is not uniformity and order but the reconciliation and fulfillment of creation's rich diversity. God's unity is one of movement rather than static structure, and the unity of selfhood one has in response to God's unity is an orientation rather than a list of specifications. "The oneness which the God of Jesus Christ demands in us is not the integration of our purposes and values but our integrity, singleness of mind and purity of heart."[12]

Power is as much a part of our religious imagination as is unity. Our own powerlessness in the face of the final reality upon which we are absolutely dependent often raises the question of God in the first place. Yet it is this final reality, this seemingly hostile or indifferent power, that Jesus speaks of as Father. The power we had expected deity to vanquish is God's own power. And what is more startling, the power struggle is won by weakness and self-sacrifice. Our religious knowledge undergoes a considerable shock when the power of God is embodied in Jesus, "the meek and dying life which through death is raised to power."[13]

Faith, as confidence and loyalty, demands that its object be valuing and valuable. Deity must bestow *goodness* and itself be a good worth seeking. The God revealed in Jesus Christ fulfills the latter requirement in a strange way. We are met by a concern that precedes our own, a god that loves before it is loved, an active seeking-out rather than a passive waiting-to-be-worshiped. This transformation in our vision of God's intrinsic goodness initiates a revolution in our understanding of God's instrumental goodness. We are God's instruments in the service of goods that are God's and not our own.

> The self we loved is not the self God loves, the neighbors we did not prize are his treasures. . . . He requires of us the sacrifice of all we would conserve and grants us gifts we had not dreamed of. . . . [14]

Those to whom God has been revealed as First Person, those who know themselves to be known by the infinite Thou, can never return to their original starting point. They have entered a new stage in their most fundamental relation; they have set out upon a course of reconciliation for themselves and society. The self who responds to the One in and beyond the many in faith and thereby acknowledges social solidarity with all selves is already a participant in the permanent revolution initiated and sustained by God's revelation in Jesus Christ.

CREATOR AND REDEEMER

Niebuhr's understanding of the One in and beyond the many as First Person identifies universal power and order with reconciliation. God the Creator is God the Redeemer. This is evident in Niebuhr's interpretation of sin and salvation.

In the face of the divisiveness and conflict that mark selfhood in its relational context, we are likely to mistake the basis of *sin*. We are apt to believe that sin is located in particular individuals or classes which we then feel obliged to eliminate or restrain: if only we could defeat the president or control the Communists, then things would be all right. We may believe that sin is rooted in evil institutions: if we could just get rid of the bureaucratic state or the church hierarchy, then people could trade according to their needs and commune together freely. We might be convinced that sin is the manifestation of our prolonged but waning adolescence: if we could only perfect education, technology, and group therapy, we would finally reach maturity. There is, of course, an implied elitism or moralism in all of these assessments. If there are "bad guys," then there must be "good guys," e.g., the opposition candidate or the capitalists, the libertarians or the sectarians, the educators, technocrats, and psychotherapists. More serious than the arbitrary identification of sin and sinners is the superficiality of the whole analysis. Sin, as Niebuhr understands it, is fundamentally a problem between us and God. Conduct aimed at overcoming sin on any basis short of the God-person relation simply heightens divisiveness and conflict.

The realization that sin is rooted in our relation to God need not begin with personal feelings of guilt or theological doctrines of the church. It can begin simply by observing the objective configurations of trust and loyalty that undergird divisiveness and conflict. "We observe that men are primarily loyal to themselves, to their nations, to their pleasure, to their race, to their machines, etc."[15] It is this loyalty to the gods that lies at the base of our alienation from ourselves, our contemporaries, and nature. We have seen this in the struggle among polytheistic and henotheistic forms of faith. Destructive consequences follow the competition among finite centers of value and social causes. If, with Niebuhr, we discover that personal and communal alienation ultimately lead to a last reality transcending all our patterns of trust and loyalty, then we are ready to consider his definition of sin as "the failure to worship God as God."[16]

The last reality present to us in our growing awareness of the limitations of all our finite objects of security and devotion is itself a limitation. The One beyond the many is our ultimate frustration. Niebuhr writes of three responses we make in our willingness to worship this One as God. First there are the Captain Ahabs who defy the enemy and fight to the end. They are easier to find in literature than in life. Perhaps Albert Camus' Dr. Rieux represents what many of us would like to be in the face of a scheme of things in which children are put to torture.

But we are more apt to make the second and more popular response, seeking to ignore the ultimate reality in a succession of allegiances that yield little pleasures. Our affluent society is ripe with fruits that put us to sleep. The good life with its fine food and entertainment even includes the exercise of our spirit in such enterprises as the monthly sales award or the annual school board election. As we hurry from one activity to another, a great forgetfulness overcomes us. The sharp outlines of defiance fade. The death of men and women in Africa and Appalachia becomes an issue for political debate. Our own death becomes a problem for the Mutual of Omaha representative.

But there is a third response to the enemy. It generally follows some personal crisis that shakes us awake. Niebuhr calls it appeasement. We offer gifts, tax deductible donations, and hours of volunteer service. We discipline our minds and our bodies, learning Scripture passages and jogging for Jesus. We become proficient in the cultivation of guilt-consciousness. But all these responses—the defiance, the forgetfulness, and the appeasement—are responses to the great destroyer, the hidden, hostile God. "In sin man lives before God—unknown as God, unknown as good, unrecognized as loveworthy and loving."[17]

If sin is the failure to worship God as God, *salvation* is the freedom to do so. Salvation is the liberating recognition that God the enemy is God the companion. Salvation is the personal transformation from suspicion to trust. "The struggle of faith and despair, the reconciliation of God and man, the victory of a faith that relies on the last, the ultimate power of being, the crucifixion and the resurrection of the self with Christ are enacted in the living self."[18] The mystery at the heart of this transformation— this great reconciliation—is ultimately impenetrable, and Niebuhr attempts only to describe something of the dynamics involved.

Central to Niebuhr's understanding of sin and salvation is *creation.*

> The doctrine of creation is the presupposition of the doctrine of sin. The latter doctrine implies that man's fundamental nature, obscured and corrupted though it is, is perfect. His perfection as a creature, or his health, is not a far-off achievement, a more or less remote possibility which future generations may realize after infinite effort; it is rather the underlying datum of life.[19]

All too often the implication of created goodness is lost in the concentration on sin. Revelation as transforming power is the event that puts us in touch with our created goodness, our primary relation to God. Here again we see the significance of Niebuhr's belief that all women and men exist and move and have their being in God. We are responding to God in everything that we do whether we know it or not. The sovereignty of God is not established in revelation, it is demonstrated there. We are transformed in the recognition of God's presence, in the awareness that the principle of being is good. There is more to the created order than persons and nature. The Creator is present, and we only become fully human in faithful relation to that One in and beyond the many.

Niebuhr's doctrine of creation is inseparable from his Christology. In Christ we see the character of the universe. We discover the identity of God the Creator and God the Redeemer. "The Word that became flesh and dwelt among us, the Son who does the work of the Father in the world of creation, has entered into a human culture that has never been without his ordering action."[20] God-in-Christ is the Creator redeeming creation. Christ-in-God is the Redeemer creating the universe for fulfillment. When a self makes this identification with personal immediacy, the transforming power of revelation has been and is effective.

When the created order takes on meaning in Jesus Christ, we experience the transformation of things already known and felt. We still respond to nature and to causes, but natural phenomena are no longer alien and relations of commitment are no longer distracting. This is not to equate "whatever is, is good" with "whatever is, is right." There is still tension between the actual and the possible, and the conversion to salvation from sin is never complete. But the primary participant in the actual is God, and the substance of salvation is friendship with God. When God the enemy becomes God the companion, we experience a radical transformation.

In revelation the self discovers that the God to whom it has been responding all along has already been active on its behalf. The Christological identification of creation and redemption expresses the conversion experience of being found, of having already been accepted. The transforming power of revelation is not the power of positive thinking whereby we say that the basic fact of life is our sin, and therefore we can save ourselves. It is the power of the divine presence whereby we say that the basic fact of life is God's creation, and therefore we cannot save ourselves.

From Niebuhr's perspective, the *fall* is seen as a perversion of creation. It is neither the absence nor the extension of the created order. The fall takes place now. Like the story of creation, the story of the fall is about our present situation. We are turning away from our created goodness, our primary relation to God. The search for self-understanding and guidance is continually misdirected by those who have chosen self-sufficiency over completion in God. The search for group identity and direction is continually detoured by institutions that have opted for structure and status over communication and community. In this fallen situation, attempts at self-salvation emphasize sin rather than the creation sin distorts. Like the attempts of nations that seek peace through war, they are destined to fail.

The denial of the Creator, while remaining absolutely dependent upon the power and order of creation, results in the self-contradiction that characterizes sin. Persons and nations contradict their very being by responding to wealth and might rather than the Creator. Christians and churches contradict their very being by responding to self-will and public opinion rather than the spirit of creation. The self-contradictory nature of these responses is underscored by comparison with the responses of Jesus Christ. In his steadfast responsibility to the Creator, Jesus manifests the healing, reconciling power of creation. But the persons and nations, the believers and religious bodies of Jesus' day, blinded by their own self-contradiction, hung him on a cross.

> Christ, the lover of God, loves the world; it responds to his love with rejection and hatred. . . . He comes to testify about God; the world answers, not with its corroborative testimony about its maker and redeemer, but with references to its lawgivers, its holy days and its culture. "He came unto his own and his own received him not."[21]

The transformation from self-contradiction to self-fulfillment must come from the Creator. According to Niebuhr, this is what happens in Jesus Christ, the ever-contemporary revelatory event. Again, the association of creation and Christology is striking. The radical conversion from self-centeredness to God-centeredness takes place in Jesus Christ. Jesus Christ is the representative symbol and the guiding form of creation itself. Through the transforming power of revelation we are turned around from the self-contradiction of henotheism and polytheism to the self-fulfillment of radically monotheistic faith. Revelation in its transforming power is a personal encounter between the Creator and the creature. It is the self-disclosure of God, not God the void or God the enemy but God the companion. In the Christ-event the last reality is First Person. Self and God are reconciled.

The personal revolution that takes place in revelation is liberation. To receive the gift of radically monotheistic faith is to be freed for the worship of God as the personal principle of being and value. We are released from the suffocating anxiety that accompanies mutual suspicion. The death-dealing horizon that threatens us in sin beckons to us in salvation as the continual source of new life. There is an expansiveness and openness about life lived in friendship with the Creator.

GOD AND WAR

The acknowledgment of the One in and beyond the many as First Person, the identification of Creator and Redeemer, faces a serious challenge with respect to war. In the context of World

War II Niebuhr wrote several articles that took up this challenge. Here we discover the providential, ordering character of God; we see that the Creator and Redeemer is also the Governor and Judge. "To deny that God is in war is for the monotheist equivalent to the denial of God's universality and unity—to the denial that God is God."[22]

To assert that *God acts in war* is not simply to claim that God influences our response to war through the emotional or psychological self. God is really active in natural and historical events themselves. Religious objectivism, as Niebuhr calls this understanding of the divine presence, must be ready to seek God's intention and meaning in any event. This is not to say that the search will always be successful or that it will ever be complete. The challenge is often difficult for "there is no evil in the city but the Lord has done it; no crucifixion but the One has crucified."[23] Yet to ignore or deny this challenge is to admit that things happen in the realm of being that are beyond the power and order of God. The responsible self for whom Jesus Christ is the organizing principle has no alternative but to seek God's action in and through all finite action, human and nonhuman. The question "What is going on?" becomes the question "What is God doing?"

Niebuhr underlines the distinction between "the fundamental confidence in God which forms the basis for a Christian's interpretation of any particular event" and "the special doctrines which he employs in such interpretation."[24] The radical monotheist trusts in the activity of God in all events without necessarily being able to specify that activity in all cases. He or she chooses to accept the mysterious even while exploring its depths for meaning. In the face of natural disasters and monstrous acts of inhumanity that mark our existence, the radical monotheist refuses to accept the clever interpretations of those who invent a self-satisfying, moralistic equation between the divine intention and the status quo. Likewise, the radical monotheist rejects the despair of those who, finding the observable data inconclusive or negative, terminate their search in an abyss or an always-losing battle with death. If ours is a time of war, then we must try to discover God's action in war, so that we may make a fitting response.

What is God doing in war? Niebuhr's answer is, in part, that *war is God's redemptive judgment.* The simplest sense in which war is an act of God is as a consequence of the created state of affairs. Regardless of humanity's abhorrence of war, the mutual limitations of finite selves are such that transgression is repelled. Overstepping one's proper limits in a single sphere of activity cannot be isolated from other spheres. We are not able to engage in economic aggression and counterattack without running the risk of military warfare. Furthermore, war is the consequence of a universal interrelatedness and interdependence that will not tolerate our refusal to accept the responsibilities incumbent upon us as social beings. War in this sense is an instrument of divine justice in the maintenance of order in the world. We can neither place ourselves over nor isolate ourselves from our neighbors and expect to avoid the consequences. A provincial view of social solidarity is bound to be destructive.

Niebuhr denies that war is properly interpreted as God's retributive or vindictive judgment. The severe deprivation and suffering of war seem to fall more heavily on the innocent. For many years now the peasants of developing nations have paid the price for the nationalistic, economic, and political ambitions of persons in distant capitals and elites within their own population. If war were understood as God's vengeance or retribution, then it would seem that the weak and humble are more the transgressors than their strong and proud oppressors. If war is understood, instead, as God's redemptive judgment, then it is through the suffering of the innocent that the guilty are challenged. War exhibits the cross of Christ.

Calvary and the events that preceded it display an ambiguous mixture of justice and injustice. Supposed righteousness clothes treachery and betrayal, while civil authority metes out death arbitrarily. But apparently Jesus attended to God's action in and through these events. He seems to respond less to the priests or Pilate or the angry mob than to God, the Lord of Heaven and earth, apart from whose power these people could not condemn or abdicate or destroy. Radical trust in God will not allow a separation between redemption and whatever judgment there is to be found in crucifixion. So also with war and all its indiscriminate suffering and death. The Christian responds to war as God's action and interprets the meaning of that action as judgment, in the assurance that it is somehow redemptive.

This is by no means an easy assurance. The self is continually tempted to make its primary responses to entities other than God. It interprets war in terms of national self-defense, or the establishment of democratic governments, or the achievement of peace. "Country, Democracy and Peace are surely values of a high order, if they are under God, but as rivals of God they are betrayers of life."[25] Primary and continual responsiveness to God pulls us beyond our most cherished communities and values. Not even the United States and democratic capitalism are exempt from the redemptive judgment of God.

The assurance of redemption in war falls to another temptation when its scope is limited. We may affirm God's redemptive judgment in war while actually waging the conflict primarily in response to economic, political, and strategic considerations, as though these matters were somehow outside God's realm. Oil and construction interests, popular support in the next election, and competing military or diplomatic strategies determine our responses. Yet it is Niebuhr's contention that the redemptive judgment of God is the judgment of the one universal God, not the God of spiritual life or the God of Christian worship or the God of religious institutions. The revolution initiated in Jesus Christ extends to the waging of war as well as the pious statements we make about its injustice and immorality. Paying taxes and designing weaponry are no less a response to God than hymns of praise and prayers for peace. A theological treatment of war is a radical treatment because the God-person relation transcends all others. To respond to God in war may pit son against father, citizen against nation, employee against employer.

God's redemptive judgment in war is corrective. In times of crisis individuals and communities are faced with the serious injustice of artificial racial and religious barriers. Arbitrary political, economic, and social distinctions are seen as perversions rather than preservers of personal and national health. In wartime action is taken to overcome these barriers. Such efforts, though never completely and permanently effective, exemplify a renewed awareness of moral issues.

Perhaps such causes as self-determination among workers, civil rights for blacks, and equal opportunities for women were advanced in part because of the problems and possible solutions that came to light during World War II. How Niebuhr would have interpreted God's corrective judgment in the United States' war in Vietnam is a matter of speculation. One might argue that war tore our nation apart, increasing rather than decreasing the tragic disparities between employer and employee, between black and white, between male and female. But perhaps the correction in question was more radical. Perhaps the war was judgment on a way of life that breeds not only affluence and comfort, but fear, violence, and exploitation. Some frantic efforts to erase all memory of Vietnam may be in response to that judgment.

Even if war is understood as God's action to maintain universal order or reorient deeply perverted human energies, one is still left with the fact that this is accomplished at the expense of millions of innocent lives. *War is crucifixion.* We can discuss war at our dinner tables; we can debate its meaning in our classrooms; we can consider its consequences on our TV panels. But here in the United States our homes are not in flames; our schools are not evacuated; our lines of communication are not being bombed.

> The maintenance of order in the universe and the internal correction of the justice of groups at war is accomplished, it is apparent, at the cost of individuals and of special people who are not maintained or corrected but slain. And some of them, we must admit, are apparently spiritually maimed even more than physically. They feel forsaken of God and they descend to the abyss. These facts about war are religiously the most difficult.[26]

Here again Niebuhr resorts to the symbolic form of Jesus Christ and the vicarious suffering of his crucifixion. In war God acts upon us in the maiming, death, and despair of many suffering servants. The Christian responds to this action as the first Christians responded to the death of Jesus Christ. This suffering on the part of creatures is as well the priceless sacrifice of the Creator to which men and women must respond in coming to understand the true order of the universe.

> Yet how the divine grace appears in the crucifixion of war may become somewhat clear when the cross of Christ is used to interpret it. Then our attention is directed to the death of the guiltless, the gracious, and the suffering of the innocent becomes a call to repentance, to a total revolution of our minds and hearts. And such a call to repentance—not to sorrow but to spiritual revolution—is an act of grace, a great recall from the road to death which we all travel together, the just and the unjust, the victors and the vanquished.[27]

The trust that undergirds this interpretation of God's action in crucifixion and in war is the confidence that servant and served alike are participants in a process of universal redemption. This is not a rationalistic confidence. It is a confidence given in the face of war as it was once and is now given in the face of a cross. It is faith that the One who slays will resurrect, that the One who destroys will recreate.

To speak of war as crucifixion or as God's redemptive judgment is extremely difficult after Auschwitz. The systematic destruction of European Jewry is a horror that transcends World War II and other wars as well. Auschwitz is the greatest challenge to Niebuhr's notion of redemptive suffering. The responsible Christian cannot use that notion to justify in any way the death of six million Jews. If Niebuhr is correct, one can instead bring the suffering of Auschwitz to expression in acts of reconciliation, trusting in the God who suffered there as at Golgotha.

In assessing God's action in war, Niebuhr does not forget that *women and men act in war*. There is no war without human intention and participation. "The immediate occasion for every war is given by some act of human faithlessness."[28] We have seen the fundamental significance of interpersonal and intercommunal commitments in maintaining the social fabric of human existence. When promises are broken, the fabric is weakened;

when we habitually act in expectation of bad faith, the fabric is torn, perhaps beyond repair.

The diplomatic quest for a negotiated settlement in Vietnam, no less than the military quest for victory, was a saga of suspicion and deceit. Behind the mutual distrust among men and women lies distrust of God. Once we reject the goodness of the reality that brackets our life at beginning and end, we must secure our own existence. This futile task puts us over against nature and our contemporaries. It requires new commitments, but now they are divisive or exclusive. Finite objects of faith and limited causes command the trust and loyalty intended for God.

> War cannot be analyzed as the simple outcome of idolatry, to be sure, but the idolatry of man in days of peace is a precondition of war and the idolatry of man at war inflames the passions of conflict and lengthens the struggle.[29]

Understood from the perspective of Christian responsibility, war offers a perverted manifestation of trust and loyalty. We often wage war to keep faith with other citizens or allies. Comrades in arms may have been enemies in some previous conflict, but now they fight together for a common cause. War reveals the depth of the human capacity for devotion and self-sacrifice. Yet all this selfless commitment covers a profound disloyalty and lack of confidence. The faith that life is worth living is present here, but squandered on the gods rather than God. It leads to alienation instead of reconciliation, war instead of peace.

War is a dramatic exhibition of sin, but Christian responsibility calls attention to something more basic. The revolutionary person tries to respond to the Creator rather than to distorted acts of creatures. With Jesus Christ as symbolic form, as organizing principle, the responsible Christian seeks in every action, even the hostile actions of the enemy, the "universal being and action which Jesus called Father."[30] In this exercise of Christian responsibility, women and men must not forget that they themselves are free and accountable participants in the dialogue. Finding God in the world and its wars is not the same thing as playing God.

It is not easy to maintain the single-minded attention to God that characterizes Jesus' sonship. As in the first century, so in the twentieth, we are distracted by the weakness and confusion of our leaders, the professional pulpiteering and patriotic moralism of our religious and political institutions. In war the complex relational interaction that continually challenges our personal integrity is especially evident.

In war we may even be distracted by our own sacrifices. Whether our life is disrupted in waging war or protesting it, we are liable to mistake our own suffering for the vicarious suffering of the innocent. Self-righteousness blurs the distinction between our will and God's. Here Niebuhr's call for objectivism is all-important. We must begin with the facts of our own experience. Vietnamese peasants who wanted only to be left in peace and American sons who had no desire to be drafted were killed or maimed or psychologically damaged for no apparent fault of their own. "Then we need to say, because we see it to be true, that whether they do so willingly or unwillingly, the innocent suffer for our sins; then we need to respond to our understanding of human tragedy as those who turn away with loathing from their own sin."[31] Our recognition of the vicarious suffering of the innocent is a recognition of universal social solidarity and our own accountability for the destructive provincialism of war.

We may avoid mistaking our sacrifices for those of the innocent and yet confuse our warfaring activity with the activity of God. So it is that we continue the development and deployment of nuclear weapons in the name of peace. We are prone to identify God's intention with our own. Again Niebuhr's objectivism operates as a corrective. If our will is God's, why do we proclaim the transgression of our opponents rather than take stock of our own short-comings? If our will is God's, why does the restitution of internal injustice follow rather than precede the necessities of war? We may be objects of divine justice in war, but we are clearly not its administrators. "God does not act save through finite instruments but none of the instruments can take the place of God even for a moment."[32]

In Christian responsibility, then, the self interprets war as

God's redemptive judgment. It refrains from those relative judgments of its own that serve only to heighten the conflict. Instead of seeking self-justification in comparison with its enemies, the self measures its own faithlessness against the faithfulness of God. Placing its trust and loyalty in God and abandoning itself and its nation as the ultimate value-center and cause, the self is freed from defensiveness in its judgments and actions. It responds to God's redemptive judgment by seeking reconciliation. The self tries to bring together what war tears apart. Though it is not inconceivable that this will entail further warfare, that prospect carries the risk of nuclear holocaust. What form the redemptive judgment of God could possibly take in the wake of such an event *is* inconceivable.

CHAPTER IV

Community

Revelation initiates and sustains a permanent revolution of the mind and heart. The transition from God the enemy to God the companion is liberation from distrust of the One in and beyond the many. It is the gift of freedom to respond to the promise of life rather than the threat of death. Delivered from the tyranny of temporal gods and closed societies, one's actions are shaped into "an interaction moving always toward universal, eternal life."[1] It can be said with equal fairness to Niebuhr's religious thought that revelation initiates and sustains a revolutionary community of radically monotheistic faith. In what sense is this community religious, and how is it to be identified with the Christian tradition?

RELIGION AND CHRISTIANITY

In Niebuhr's work the term "religion" carries one of three meanings depending on the context. We encountered the first sense of religion in our discussion of faith. The religious question is the question of life's meaning. Men and women have a religious need for something that makes their life worth living. The gods, as objects of trust and loyalty, fill this need.

In this first sense, religion and faith are closely related, if not synonymous, terms. Religion, "as the faith that life is worth living, as the reference of life to a source of meaning and value, as the practice of adoration and worship," is common to all persons.[2] However, when the word "faith" is used to refer to the triadic structures manifest in a variety of human activities, not all of which are directly concerned with the source of life's meaning and value, it is appropriate to distinguish between religion and faith. This is also in order when faith designates primitive confidence in general, only one aspect of which is related to our existence as worshiping beings. As knowing, moral beings we exhibit this fundamental faith as confidence in the intelligibility of nature and in one another.

Given these distinctions, the "religious aspect of faith," or simply "religious faith," refers to those particular manifestations of trust and loyalty directly involved with the source of life's ultimate meaning and value. Religion, so understood, is a pervasive force affecting all human activity. It is an integrating factor that defines or apprehends the final context in which particular self-actions are significant. Thus Niebuhr believes that "the reformation of religion is the fundamental reformation of society."[3]

Niebuhr uses the term "religion" in two other senses. Religion as piety includes elements such as the sense of the holy, prayer, and ecstasy. Religion also refers to such organized movements in history as Judaism and Islam.[4] In neither of these uses is religion synonymous with faith. In the first instance the reference is to a particular kind of human experience and activity. In the second instance the reference is to a loose community of persons engaged in a variety of activities. In both cases we are dealing with something that is formed and transformed by faith. So it is that piety and organized religion exhibit conflict among the forms of faith.

Each of the three meanings of religion has an appropriate use with respect to Christianity. Christianity is an organized religion. It is a loose community in which the focus of numerous and varied activities is Jesus Christ. One of these activities, sometimes the dominant one, is the practice of religion as piety. Christian communities gather to share the experience of the holy, join in prayers of confession and intercession, and celebrate God's active presence. Most importantly, Jesus Christ, the transforming power and organizing principle in Christianity, points to the Lord of heaven and earth in answer to the question of life's ultimate meaning.

As Niebuhr himself likes to speak of it, Christianity has its identity in terms of its primary symbolic forms and its cause.

Thus, the Christian is a follower of Jesus Christ. As such, the Christian is included in that

> community of men for whom Jesus Christ—his life, words, deeds and destiny—is of supreme importance as the key to the understanding of themselves and their world, the main source of the knowledge of God and man, good and evil, the constant companion of the conscience, and the expected deliverer from evil.[5]

If one is a follower of Jesus Christ, one identifies oneself more or less with the cause of Jesus Christ, which Niebuhr designates as the reconciliation of men and women to God. The community as well as the individual is identified in terms of this cause. It is "a people chosen for service in bearing witness to the One beyond all the many, elected to live by, and to mediate to others, confidence in the principle of being itself and loyalty to its cause."[6]

Whether we attend to the individual or the community, whether we speak of symbolic form or the cause in which it issues, in Christianity we are dealing with a movement. The transformation of the self and the reinterpretation of its manifold relations is a permanent revolution of the mind and heart. So, too, Christianity as a community of revolutionary persons is embarked upon a continual transformation of society and a constant reinterpretation of its priorities. It is a revolutionary movement informed by Jesus Christ and committed to the task of establishing friendship between God and persons, of reconciling men and women to one another and to their natural environment. In a fallen and ever-changing world, this task is never complete.

In citing as the task of the Christian movement the reconstruction of confidence in the Creator and allegiance to the creation, Niebuhr is not suggesting that such a revolution takes place only in and through Christianity. Radical faith does exist where Christianity is not present, and, all too obviously, the presence of Christianity often obstructs rather than encourages universal community. It should also be noted that Niebuhr's identification of Christianity in terms of a symbolic form as well as a cause does not imply that there is a Christian God and that Jews and Moslems are necessarily attending to a different God. There is a Christian relation to God, and where that relation is actualized,

Jesus Christ is the mediator of radically monotheistic faith. Such reconciliation in our most fundamental relation is revolutionary for the individual and for society. When Christianity is vital, it is the scene of this revolution and the movement in history from which it spreads.

THE CHURCH

The church is the social reality that embodies the Christian movement. In an effort to do justice to its dynamic character, Niebuhr sets forth his most extended definition of the church in terms of a polar analysis. He begins with *subject and object.* The church is the "subjective pole of the objective rule of God."[7] The object of the church as apprehending subject is God. "Object" in its use here does not deny the personal, subject character of God. It affirms the otherness of God, the distinction between the church and God. Attempting to be neither God nor God's kingdom, the church accepts the psychological, historical, and religious relativism that characterizes any finite community. Put most simply, where selves apprehend God and participate in God's cause, there is the church.

> For what is the church save the assembly of people before God, or the movement of those who, abandoning all relative and finite goals, turn toward the infinite end of life? It is the *ecclesia* which has been called out of the pluralism and the temporalism of the world to loyalty to the supreme reality and only good, on which the goodness of all finite things depends.[8]

The uniqueness of the church is not that it is related to the final reality but that it is reconciled to that reality. The particular relation of the church to the One on whom it and all else is absolutely dependent is inseparable from Jesus Christ. This community of reconciliation is, therefore, the Christian church, though more importantly, it is the church of God. In taking its stand with Jesus Christ, it points away from itself and away from Jesus Christ to the Lord of heaven and earth. From such a stance the church acknowledges its relation to and its distinction from all other communities related to the One in and beyond the many.

To assert that the church exists where the One beyond the

many is apprehended as God, and to further assert that the
church's reconciled relation to God is inseparable from Jesus
Christ, might seem to suggest that there is no reconciliation that
does not take place through Jesus Christ. Niebuhr is unwilling
to put the matter so simply. An earlier quotation is worth repeating here:

> I do not have the evidence which allows me to say that the mir-
> acle of faith in God is worked only by Jesus Christ and that it is
> never given to men outside the sphere of his working, though I
> may say that where I note its presence I posit the presence also
> of something like Jesus Christ.[9]

With respect to the church a similar statement would be appropriate. Niebuhr is not concerned to define the precise limits
of the church, nor is any theologian equipped to identify all instances and degrees of reconciliation. The point is that Christianity is essentially a movement of reconciliation between persons
and God. Where such reconciliation takes place in two or more
selves, there we posit the presence of something like the church.

The second polarity Niebuhr uses in defining the church is
that of *community and institution*. The church is a common confidence and loyalty, a compelling spirit of reconciliation. The
church is also disciplines and rituals, denominations, boards and
agencies. The church is both a structured community and a spirit-
filled institution. Thus Niebuhr can speak of an invisible ecumenical movement that is at once the precondition for and the
result of developing ecumenical institutions. Though either the
community or the institutional pole may be emphasized in
describing the church or participating in it as a social reality,
neither pole is adequate by itself.

A slightly different version of the community-institution polarity in Niebuhr's work is the church of faith and the religious
institutions called churches. The church of faith is "an eschatological society" belonging to that order of existence which "can
neither be described in temporal terms nor abstracted from the
temporal."[10] It is an emergent reality present in the churches but
not to be identified with them. Insofar as the churches are the
objects of conversion and the scenes of reconciliation, they are

participants in the universal fellowship of faith. In awareness of and service to the true church of faith as already present and in hope for its full emergence, the churches are themselves revolutionary forces in the world.

The polarity between *unity and plurality* is also to be found in the church. While unified in its allegiance to the One beyond the many, the church offers diverse expressions of its loyalty. Its many members are unique yet interdependent participants in one body. The rich pluralism that is the church has its integrity in response to the oneness of God; a complete analysis of the church must take cognizance of both poles. "Interest in unity opens our eyes to unitive elements in the church's life; it limits our vision at the same time; other embodied values, particularly those connected with diversity and with conflict do not come into view."[11] Far too many churches illustrate by their homogeneity the difficulty of maintaining the polarity of unity and plurality.

Locality and universality constitute a fourth polarity in which the church exists. We tend to think of the church in terms of churches, local congregations in their particularity, significant or insignificant among other social realities. But in its faith in the One in and beyond the many the local church is related to every other congregation in a universal community of faith. The self and its social companions in Jesus Christ express and represent a process of reconciliation that has no regional boundaries.

The church is both *protestant and catholic*. It is protestant in its recognition of the relativity of all existents before the One beyond the many. It protests against any confusion of the infinite with the finite, the transcendent with the immanent, the eternal with the temporal. The church is catholic in its recognition of the worth of all existents relative to the One in as well as beyond the many. It affirms the representation of the infinite in the finite, the activity of the transcendent in the immanent, the manifestation of the eternal in the temporal.

Unity and plurality, locality and universality, protestant and catholic—these polarities illustrate with respect to the church some of the primary themes in Niebuhr's religious thought. There is no good but God, yet everything that is, is good in relation to

God. There is no deed the Lord has not done, yet every person stands accountable for his or her acts. There is no adequate description for the One beyond the many, yet this One's presence is more immediate than that of our most cherished friend. The church has no alternative but to exist in the midst of a restless peace. It knows that its particular being is only part of the whole, yet without it the whole would be different. It knows that its projects are partial and often badly flawed, yet others are depending on its activity. It knows that nothing it does is sufficient, yet if it does nothing, a tremendous opportunity has been missed.

The final polarity Niebuhr uses in setting forth a definition of the church is that of *church and world*. Here, as in the subject-object polarity with which we began, the church itself is one of the poles. The church-world distinction is neither as fundamental nor as clear cut as that between church and God. The church's relation to God determines its relation to the world and its distinction from the world. In turning to the principle of being as God, the church acknowledges its relation to all existents, individual and corporate. Furthermore, it acknowledges that the character of its relation to the world is one of concern and service. In responding to God the church becomes responsible for the world. Trust in the principle of being entails loyalty to the realm of being. The priority of the subject-object or the church-God polarity and its influence on the character of the church-world polarity is a manifestation of the double movement characteristic of any triad of faith and eminently exhibited in Jesus Christ's relation to God and to persons.

It is devotion to God that turns the self or the community back into the world. The significance of this double movement is not the creation of a church-world relation that had not existed previously but the reorientation of that relation before God. The church as a finite social reality is trustworthy. The reconciliation of God and persons is taking place, however haltingly, in the church. The church, identifying itself vis-à-vis God, is keenly aware that it is world and not God, but this awareness is no longer cause for despair. The church is distinct from the world in its assurance that the enemy of all worldly gods is a friend.

> Though it sounds paradoxical it seems nevertheless to be true
> that the important difference between the church and the world
> is that the church knows itself to be "world" before God while
> the world does not know this but thinks that it can be like God.
> Perhaps it would be better to say that the church consists of that
> portion of humanity which, knowing God, knows that man is not
> God and has made the decision before God that it will not play
> God but let God be Lord.[12]

The church-God relation continually dictates change and development in the church-world relation. The result is a broad
pattern of alternation between withdrawal and aggression. When
the church is so bound by worldly interests that it can no longer
serve the world, then it must withdraw in order to renew its
primary covenant with God and reawaken that other-worldly interest that motivates this-worldly service. This withdrawal pro-
pels the church back into the world where it can now recognize
the real sources of redemption and salvation, the emergent kingdom its little trusts and its exclusive loyalties had concealed. This
pattern manifests on a corporate and historically extended scale
the double movement of the triad of faith.

Niebuhr's own writing about the church exhibits this pattern
of withdrawal and aggression. His early essays call for separation
from the world:

> The pendulum has swung about as far as it may toward this-
> worldliness. . . . The old monastic virtues need to be over-
> emphasized if they are to make a sufficient impression upon a
> time which has almost completely forgotten them.
>   The first of these virtues is the virtue of an undivided interest
> in the spiritual world, conceived as standing in opposition to the
> present world.[13]

Pointing out the bondage to humanism, nationalism, and capitalism, Niebuhr urges the church to seek its independence.[14]
But as new circumstances develop out of the corruption and conversion that mark human history, Niebuhr's emphasis gradually
shifts. Midway in his career he notes two kinds of irresponsibility
in the church-world relation. The wordly church inverts its responsibility to God for society and becomes responsible to society for God. The isolated church is responsible to God, but for

itself rather than society.[15] More and more it is to the latter form of irresponsibility that Niebuhr reacts.

> A consequence of the decision in our time . . . to define the church in opposition to the world has been the tendency to ignore or deprecate the "worldly" character of the church and the "churchly" character of the world . . . to cultivate a church life in separation from the world.[16]

So it is that in an article written in 1960 Niebuhr seeks a reformation in the church "not now by separation from the world but by a new entrance into without conformity to it."[17]

The remarkable aspect of this development in Niebuhr's thought about the church and the world is its constant dependence upon his understanding of the church-God relation and the double movement that relation entails. In the midst of his call for liberation of the church from its bondage to civilization, he reminds us that "such an emancipation can be undertaken only for the sake of a new aggression and a new participation in constructive work."[18] Radically monotheistic faith attends to God for its orientation in the changing world. It responds to God throughout a church-world history that is never fixed. "In the faith of the church, the problem is not one of adjustment to the changing, relative, and temporal elements in civilization but rather one of constant adjustment, amid these changing things, to the eternal."[19]

PERMANENT REVOLUTION

As individuals and as communities, Christians and churches are engaged in a permanent revolution of selves and societies. The dynamics of this revolution are manifest in Niebuhr's understanding of ethics and the responsible church.

The double movement we have seen repeatedly in Niebuhr's work appears again in the relation between theology and ethics. Religious faith is attached to a cause or center of value that gives meaning to specific actions. Our discussions of responsibility have revealed the importance of interpretive contexts dictated by the gods. Religion is our concern for the ultimate context in which actions are fitting. So it is that theology and ethics are distinct but inseparable. Theology without ethics becomes dogmatic and ineffective. Ethics without theology becomes rudderless in the winds and currents of culture.[20]

Niebuhr's own work exhibits the interrelation of theology and ethics. Considerations of divine action are coupled with attention to fitting human response, and discussions of social-cultural action are placed in the context of the God-person relation. Niebuhr's interpretation of war is a striking example. In our present consideration of the church we can see how ethics, like theology, is itself a communal expression of the God-person relation. The self whose personal identity and integrity of action in relation to God is through the mediation of Jesus Christ finds himself or herself at work in the world in community with others who relate to God through the same symbolic form. The ethics that emerges from this situation reflects the mutual interaction that characterizes the triad of God, self, and community. It serves to summarize many of the themes discussed in this interpretive exposition of Niebuhr's work.

Evangelical ethics refers to the "positive movement and orientation of the Christian life."[21] Of its four primary characteristics, the first is *theocentricity*.

> The chief descriptive statement which can be made about this Evangelical ethics is that it is the mode of life which issues out of a positive relation to God, as that relation is established by, through, and with Jesus Christ. It is *theocentric* ethics. It is the ethics which accompanies a dominant orientation of the self and the community toward the action of God.[22]

Niebuhr's interpretation of war as the judgment of God is an instance of this theocentric orientation. In war the Christian responds to the activity of a living God, not simply the threats of other combatants.

The Christian ethicist must take care not to substitute a finite mediator of divine action for the divine agent. Church-centered or Bible-centered ethics exemplify this danger in a legalism that restricts and distorts the redemptive spirit of God. Another danger lies in preoccupation with negative counterparts of God's glory and grace. If ethics begins with sin and the inability to achieve our own salvation, it is likely to fall into defensiveness or despair. The ethicist who strives above all else to be "realistic" with respect to "human nature" may in fact give an inadequate account of our primary and inescapable relation to God. This might account for the surprising number of professional Christian ethicists who advocated America's military policies in Vietnam. Be that as it may, "Evangelical ethics is God-centered, not sin-centered."[23] When we begin with our sin no less than when we begin with our righteousness, we fail to see the ever-new possibilities that come with faith in God.

Evangelical ethics is a mode of life that issues from *faith in God*. This second characteristic is rooted in the significance of trust and loyalty as the fundamental bases of human decision and action. "The conduct of life issues out of the central faith, not as conclusions are drawn from premises but as fruit derives from trees."[24] Faith may exert its influence at such a primitive level that the self is unconscious of its consequences and declares a neutrality that is actually unavailable. There can be no faithless ethics. Conduct that is not rooted explicitly or implicitly in God is necessarily idolatrous. "Hence the great ethical question is always the question of faith, 'In what does man trust?' "[25]

As with the theocentricity of ethics so with its foundation in faith, there is always the danger of perversion. Theories about faith, propositions concerned with trust and loyalty, value-centers and causes are themselves liable to become the objects of faith. Then too it is possible that the self will become so enamored of faith that it will forget faith's object. It will cultivate a subjective condition rather than an objective relation. It will come to think that faith rather than God is its salvation. The dangers of legalism and antinomianism are combated by revelation in which the transformation of faith is its attachment to God. In Evangelical ethics conduct issues not from faith but from faith in God. In the following quotation Niebuhr brings together the first two features of Evangelical ethics in a concise statement of the meaning and effect of the revelatory event.

> The recognition of this deep connection between conduct and faith is mated then with the understanding that the reformation

of faith is the reformation of life and that the great work of Christ for moral beings is his work as the renewer and transformer of faith. He redeems us by reconciling us to God, by winning us out of our distrust and fear of the Holy One, by drawing us away from our despairing trust in idols and in self. Faith in God is the gift of God through Jesus Christ and with that faith all things are given, including the transformation of human conduct.[26]

The *freedom* that arises from the self's reconciliation to God is a third aspect of Evangelical ethics. "Where faith in God is present the self is free from concern for itself."[27] It is liberated from the suffocating restrictions of self-protection and defensiveness. This freedom might simply be exchanged for a bondage to cultural value-centers were it not based on faith in the One in and beyond the many for whom the entire universe is the realm of freedom. Familial, political, and ecclesiastical boundaries insurmountable to the henotheist and mutually confusing to the polytheist are opened up to the radical monotheist.

The freedom of Evangelical ethics is also a liberation from the law that characterizes the self's distrustful relation to God. The law remains, but it is radically transformed when its bondage is exchanged for loyalty to God. What was our own demand on grudging slaves becomes the loving Parent's imperative for obedient sons and daughters. What divided according to artificial distinctions of race and status unites according to the universal grace of the principle of being. So the freedom of Evangelical ethics is a freedom *to* as well as a freedom *from*. Reconciliation with God is the self's liberty to love his or her neighbor and to do the fitting act in situations that continually confound established practices and values. Human creativity is unleashed in response to the divine creativity that is never seen by the suspicious eye. "Evangelical ethics appears as a mode of life in freedom which, though impossible to man, is being made possible by God."[28]

The freedom we have been discussing is the freedom to act now. This is an awesome possibility to those of us who have made a vocation out of waiting. We say we need more information, yet we have known all along what the situation demands of us. We

say we will act as soon as our children are grown, though we
know they despise our inaction. And then one day we are star-
tled to hear ourselves say we would act now if only it weren't
too late.

Faith in God is faith in One whose activity is not limited to
some future state of affairs. God is Lord of the present as well as
the future. God is the One in whom present and future have
their meaningful connection. Thus Niebuhr writes, "the Evangelical mode of life may be described as *momentary* in character."[29] This fourth characteristic of Evangelical ethics does not
contradict Niebuhr's frequent appeal to the significance of the
context for particular acts. Rather it affirms that because the entire context is rooted in the power and love of God, the self is
free to make the fitting response to God in the present. To say
Evangelical ethics is momentary is to say that the Christian self
has the liberty as well as the responsibility to act now.

Evangelical ethics combines the theocentric orientation of
universal responsibility with the liberating power of revelation.
In keeping with the symbolic form of Jesus Christ, the revolutionary self attempts to make each deed part of the "continuous
action which is redemptive rather than defensive."[30] Such efforts
are based upon faith in God whose activity is a present reality.
Evangelical ethics works in the confidence that the kingdom of
God is at hand. It trusts in the presence of "an ordering and
sustaining process that underlies our whole life in freedom just
as an ordering, sustaining process of nature working toward health
underlies all of our physical activities."[31] To be reconciled to God
in Jesus Christ is to understand that the orderer and sustainer is
gracious. This reconciliation relieves the frustrating tension that
accompanies the self's distortion of its relation to God. In its place
there is a creative tension that seeks an ever-greater realization
of God's kingdom on earth. This is the motivating force behind
radically monotheistic efforts to transform culture and achieve
universal community.

Such a transformation is not the work of individuals. It is the
task of relational selves, social companions in a community that
is itself theocentric, faithful, free, and momentary. Evangelical

ethics is the ethics of a church that seeks to deepen and extend the reconciliation that is its own foundation. The goal of the church is the "increase among men of the love of God and neighbor."[32] This increase is the reconstitution of social relations in accordance with a created order that is redemptive. The church is a revolutionary community in which the self can find its identity and begin to satisfy its drive for integrity. The liberation and fulfillment of social selfhood involves a transformation of society.

The same responsibility symbolism that Niebuhr employs for self-understanding and guidance is also useful in analyzing and shaping the church's activity in the world. To whom or what does the church respond, and in what community of interaction is it so responsive? The church's primary response is to God, the principle of being, and this responsiveness takes place within the world, the realm of being. The church responds in all of its relations in light of its fundamental relation to God. It interprets all finite action upon it as the action of the One beyond the many. Insofar as the church is responsible as well as responsive, it anticipates the reaction of that One to its response. In responding to and anticipating the further response of the principle of being, the church acknowledges the universal extension of its social solidarity. The church is accountable to God for the consequences of all its actions in the world.

Responsibility symbolism provides a formal structure in which to relate God, church, and world, and to see the scope of the church's accountability to God. It is in terms of another symbolic form, Jesus Christ, that the church understands the nature or character of its accountability. The transforming and organizing effect of God's revelation in Jesus Christ is the same at the corporate level of church and world as it is at the level of self and social companion. Insofar as the church is explicitly Christological in its universal responsibility, it responds to God-in-Christ and Christ-in-God.

When Niebuhr writes of *God-in-Christ*, he is referring to the fact that in the early church, and in the contemporary churches that are alive, the response to Jesus' life and death is a response to something more than Jesus. As the representative Thou in a triad of faith, Jesus points beyond himself to the Creator, the Lord of heaven and earth. This is the basis of Jesus' authority. "There is a universal and an everlasting, a powerful, inescapable content in what he says and does."[33] In responding to God-in-Christ, the church must render account to the One in and beyond the many, the universal in the particular, the eternal in the temporal. Such accountability knows no finite limits. Identified before God-in-Christ, the neighbor is no longer a function of race, or nation, or economic status, or sex. The church lives in a neighborhood that is all-inclusive and unrestricted.

When Niebuhr writes of *Christ-in-God*, he is referring to the fact that the church looks "not only to the absolute in the finite but to the redemptive principle in the absolute."[34] In Jesus' life and death and resurrection, the church discovers that the principle of being is also the principle of value, that the Lord of heaven and earth is Parent. To confess the resurrection is to confess that God is love. So, in responding to the One *beyond* the many, the church is responding to the redemptive principle *in* the many. The content of its response must be merciful. Its task is the salvation of the world, not its destruction. The reconciling dynamic that forms the church itself must characterize its activity in the world. In its universal responsibility to the loving Creator, the church recognizes that whatever is, is good. Insofar as it acts out this recognition, it is the corporate incarnation of healing faith.

In its responsibility to God for the world, the church can err in either of two directions, becoming too worldly or isolating itself from the world. The *worldly church* confuses something for which it is responsible with that to which it is responsible. In such a situation it asks not what God requires of it, but what the nation or some other finite reality requires of God. Churchly sanction for national policies is commonplace in the United States where political conventions begin and end with prayer and where clergy ask divine blessing on particular military mission. Less obvious, but no less irresponsible, is the church's tendency to direct its trust and loyalty to humankind. Continual refinement of the intellect and an ever-increasing standard of living are admirable goals for all men and women, but humanity itself is still an exclusive object of faith, an inadequate alternative to the One beyond the many. From the perspective of loyalty to God-in-Christ, a humanistic church is no different from a nationalistic church. "The substitution of any society for the infinite and absolute God involves the Church in a kind of irresponsibility in the course of which it actually betrays the society it seeks to serve."[35]

Confusion about that to which the church is responsible leads to confusion regarding its accountability. The finite society that claims the church's loyalty also gives the church its meaning. The significance attached to preaching at the president's prayer breakfast or offering financial support for a political prisoner on trial suggests the church's temptation to worldliness. Or perhaps it is most evident in worship that is geared to social effectiveness rather than responsiveness to the real presence of *God-in-Christ*. In any case, the church that "tries to render account to men for its stewardship of religious values" has betrayed its relation to God and forfeited its revolutionary power.[36]

If the worldly church mistakes that to which it is responsible, the *isolated church* mistakes that for which it is responsible. At the opposite extreme from the irresponsibility we have been discussing, the isolated church fails to take responsibility for society. Responsive to Christ-in-God, it fails to see the extent of that redemption. It stands accountable to God, but only for itself; "it thinks of itself as the being for which it must answer and it regards the secular societies with which it lives as outside the divine concern."[37] The social entities the worldly church serves to their own disservice are left without a care by the isolated church. Such a church fails to recognize that whatever is, is good and is worthy of redemption.

The isolated church couples its disdain for the world with great concern for its own salvation. The development of specific moral practices and intellectual tenets is undertaken to promote its own sanctification while protecting it from the degrading forces of society. Individual self-righteousness and communal exclusiveness characterize the church that is responsible to God but only for itself. It becomes as defensive about its own spiritual life as the worldly church is about its social causes. While the worldly church may founder on arguments over political responsibility, the isolated church is more apt to splinter over the definition of an authentic conversion experience.

The two forms of irresponsibility in the church illustrate the dynamics of the triad of faith. Just as the responsible self must live in the midst of a double movement from self to God and God to self, so must the church have its being in a similar movement from the world to God and God to the world. "The relation to God and the relation to society must neither be confused with each other as is the case in social religion, nor separated from each other as is the case in Christian isolationism; they must be maintained in the unity of responsibility to God for the neighbor."[38]

Niebuhr offers a general description of the church's responsibility to God for human societies in terms of three functions appropriate to the Christian community. The first of these is *apostolic*. To announce the gospel to all nations is to proclaim to societies as well as to social selves that the principle of being and the principle of value are one, that the last reality confronting all persons and peoples is goodness and mercy. The church must somehow make it clear to humanity as well as individuals that real freedom comes with the promise of life rather than the threat of death. This apostolic function does not avoid repentance. "The good news about the glory of divine goodness is neither rightly proclaimed nor rightly heard if it is not combined with the bad news about the great injustice which prevails in God's world."[39] The church in the United States must call attention to redemptive possibilities open to a powerful nation that is free to act in hope rather than fear. But it must also confront this nation with its accountability for the destructive consequences of militaristic self-assertion. There is no such thing as an honorable conclusion to an unjust war.

To be the apostle of God's mercy and judgment to social groups as well as social selves requires patience and imagination. The transition from an individualistic to a social period in history challenges the church's capacity to transmit its message of reconciliation. As the form of social relationships changes, so too does the form of effective healing. Though the church will certainly speak to heads of state and the like, its primary points of contact will continue to be through the membership rather than the leadership. But this is no license to maintain traditional practices and repeat ancient expressions when they have lost their meaning and relevance.

> Responsibility to the living God requires in this case as in all others an awareness of the immediate moment and its needs, a willingness to reconstruct one's own habits in order that the neighbor's needs may be met, a readiness to depart from tradition in order that the great tradition of service may be followed.[40]

The church has a *pastoral* role to fulfill in its responsibility to God for society. Its response to Christ-in-God brings it to the side of the neglected and the oppressed. Trusting in God and free to participate in the redemption of God's creation, the church tries to cooperate with black persons in their struggle for dignity. It listens to women in their ambiguous plight, seeking to respond to them rather than to its own generalizations about them. The church actively supports migrant workers in their demands for just wages and decent working conditions, but it does so without hostility to the grower who is no less the object of God's redemptive judgment.

The church's pastoral care for these individuals forces it to recognize the corporate nature of human sin. Relational selves cannot be helped as though they were discrete atomic entities. "The Church cannot be responsible to God for men without becoming responsible for their societies. As the interdependence of men increases in industrial and technological civilization the responsibility for dealing with the great networks of interrelationship increases."[41] Cooperation with blacks in their struggle for dignity may involve an organized effort to modify a city's public transportation routes or change the membership of the local school board. Listening and responding to women may involve an effective assault on the sexist practices of one's own employer. Active support for migrant workers may involve a concerted, long-term attempt to modify existing labor and agricultural legislation.

In fulfilling its pastoral responsibility to God for society, the church must remain the community of faith in Jesus Christ. The temptation to exchange transforming power for black power or feminist power or economic power is great. When such an exchange takes place, the church loses its being as a revolutionary community of reconciliation.

Finally, the church functions as a *social pioneer*. It is the part of society most sensitive and responsive to God's action. As such it is responsible to God for society in a representative sense. It acts on behalf of society, repenting for the sins of all men and women demonstrating the trust and loyalty to God that is truly human.

When the church discovers that a war is God's judgment on the United States' self-idolatry and fear of communism, then it repents for its own and its nation's sin. Its repentance is active and moves hopefully toward actual reconciliation. It does not wait for the word from peace groups to withdraw its investments in war-related industries or to cooperate with other stockholders to end weapons production. It does not wait for the courts to declare that men and women of conscience are free to refuse military service in an immoral war. It is free to be a momentary community. Because reconciliation, not retribution, is its cause, it can honor a variety of acts within its own boundaries. And its own boundaries will become especially fluid when it takes representational responsibility for society. As a sanctuary for the conscientious objector, it may also become the meeting place for groups that operate with other symbolic forms than its own. It will become vulnerable to co-optation and consequent waves of withdrawal. It may often fear crucifixion more than it hopes in resurrection. But so long as it returns again and again to the revelatory event that is its transformation and orientation, it will remain a revolutionary community of redemption.

As Jesus Christ is a representative Thou in a triad of faith that includes God and persons, so the church is a representative community in the universal triad of faith. With Jesus Christ as its symbolic form, the church participates in the double movement of faith on the corporate level. As a social entity its embodied trust and loyalty to the Creator reflects the Creator's

faithfulness to the creation. The church as social pioneer redu-
plicates the reflective-representative character of Jesus Christ
whose love of God motivates a love for men and women that is
in fact God's love for them.

> This seems to be the highest form of social responsibility in the
> Church. It is the direct demonstration of love of God and neigh-
> bor rather than a repetition of the commandment to self and oth-
> ers. It is the radical demonstration of faith. Where this
> responsibility is being exercised there is no longer any question
> about the reality of the Church.[42]

When the relational self finds its identity and its integrity of
action in response to the One in and beyond the many, when it
attaches its faith to that One, it discovers a community of reconciliation, a body of social companions faithful to a common cause.
When Jesus Christ is the transforming power and organizing
principle in such a community, he is the self-transcending third
in a cause triad that is the church. To follow Jesus Christ is to
join a larger community and become a participant in a universal
triad of faith that includes God and the world. In this context
Jesus Christ is a representative Thou and the church is a revolutionary body seeking to extend the reconciliation of God and
persons throughout the entire community of being.

CONCLUSION

Who am I? What shall I do? How is faith in God possible? We began with these questions because they are basic, because they can be asked personally by each of us, and because Niebuhr gives us ways of asking them. We proposed to look at Niebuhr's work as a window on our own lives, our own experiences with one another and with God. In setting forth some conclusions of my own in the pages that follow, I recognize that you must accomplish a similar task for yourself. I hope you will do so in conversation with Niebuhr's writings.

RELATIONAL SELFHOOD

Niebuhr never forsakes his fundamental assumption that selfhood is relational. Our understanding of ourselves as well as others is rooted in dialogue with social companions and representative Thous. Through such dialogue, meaningful contexts are established; relationships of commitment that transcend themselves draw us into new communities of meaning.

Niebuhr's ethical framework exhibits relational selfhood in its assumption that all action is reaction. The tools of interpretation that transform reaction into responsiveness are themselves a social inheritance, and we only become responsible as we accept accountability in communities of social solidarity. Even Niebuhr's conception of faith finds its definitive paradigm in the interpersonal experience of trust and loyalty.

The foundational significance of relational selfhood in Niebuhr's religious thought gives his work relevance today, despite the massive culture shocks that separate his theological era from our own. At a time when social science may be of greater analytical value than philosophy, Niebuhr's attention to persons in community is instructive. At a time when injustice rivals epistemology as the primary challenge to theology, Niebuhr's conjunction of faith and responsibility, of radical monotheism and universal social solidarity, merits careful attention.

Because Niebuhr's theology is grounded in a careful analysis of relational selfhood, evil is also understood in that context. The systemic character of evil, its embodiment in the structures of society, is clearly revealed. To isolate evil in a single individual or group or program deepens the very chasm one seeks to bridge in reconciling selves to one another. Similarly, to separate the problem of evil from God is to compromise the ultimate universality of responsible selfhood. Either evil is understood as a phenomenon of our distorted social solidarity, or it is given a priority that denies our absolute dependence upon the One in and beyond the many.

The prominence of relational selfhood throughout Niebuhr's work has important implications for feminist theology, theology that takes seriously the full range of female as well as male experience. As the direct quotations from his writing have made clear, Niebuhr did not anticipate the sting his exclusive language would shortly have. Given his sensitivity to the power of language and the manifold consequences of symbolic form, I suspect Niebuhr would not have continued to use male pronouns when reference to women was also intended. It might be more difficult to argue conclusively that Niebuhr's personal vision of universal social solidarity did not harbor some vestige of female inferiority. Be that as it may, the logic of his position with its repeated appeal to ever more inclusive causes runs contrary to any ultimate denial of full female personhood. Indeed, Niebuhr's respect for the systemic nature of evil in the form of oppressive social structures makes us painfully aware of the struggle that lies ahead if sexism and racial discrimination are to be overcome.

In laying out so carefully the relational context in which both faith and reason have their genesis, Niebuhr raises our consciousness to the plight of women and minority persons in a society that is prone to stereotypic assumptions and individualistic solutions. In claiming priority for responsiveness over duty and purposiveness, Niebuhr anticipated, albeit unconsciously, important elements in the feminist critique of literature and moral development theory. Perhaps his concept of revelation as an event that transforms the context of relational selfhood instead of transporting individuals to other realms, real or imagined, provides useful insight for constructive feminist theology.

JESUS CHRIST AS SYMBOLIC FORM

Niebuhr uses symbolic form to express the interaction between revelation and its present context. As organizing principle and transforming power Jesus Christ at once mirrors and transforms the situation in which we find ourselves. In his single-minded devotion to God, he illustrates the pattern of universal responsibility, representing the true self/social companion/God relationship. At the same time his representation structures that relationship in the present by empowering universal responsibility on the part of his followers and providing the image whereby those followers orient themselves in their own relation to God and social companions.

This understanding of Jesus Christ as symbolic form helps us appreciate the dynamic quality of Christian worship. The reenactment of certain past events is creative as well as commemorative. In repeating the past the present is altered. The liturgical use of bread and wine is not simply an intellectual link with a sacrificial act two-thousand years old; it is also the enabling moment for the giving of one's self in the present. The invitation to all persons to gather at the table is not simply the habitual practice of thanksgiving for a historic community; it is also the reconciliation of persons presently divided by race, gender, politics, and even religion.

The liturgical appropriation of Jesus Christ as symbolic form is by no means confined to the sanctuary. The Christian is a participant in numerous triadic relationships that extend beyond or originate outside the church. The worshiping community is always in creative tension with the world of which it is also a part.

At its best it operates with the same engagement that marks the New Testament picture of Jesus Christ.

One must continually enact the model of universal responsibility in a situation that has already given shape to that model. And having enacted the model, both it and the situation are different. This process, this movement from action to model to action, is ongoing. It is what some contemporary theologians call praxis. I choose the word "model" instead of theory here, because in Niebuhr's case universal responsibility, certainly as it is illustrated in Jesus Christ, is not so much a set of principles or prescribed actions as it is a relationship with God. Like a friendship, it never comes fully to rest. Reconciliation is not a final fulfillment, but the basis for new opportunities of trust and loyalty. Niebuhr underscores this in his description of revelation as permanent revolution.

The interactive character of Jesus Christ as symbolic form is nowhere more evident than in Niebuhr's understanding of death and resurrection. Resurrection is not the denial of Jesus' death; it is the confession that Jesus' death, like his life, has transforming power in the present. If one can affirm that Jesus' death, with all its loneliness and physical pain, is nevertheless meaningful because it is a response to God for all Jesus' social companions, then death loses its most threatening power, the power of meaninglessness. Indeed, since we all must die, Jesus' life is no more than an admirable example unless his death can also be affirmed. I think this is what Niebuhr is trying to articulate theologically when he writes that the God with whom we are reconciled is the death-dealer as well as the life-giver. If that is so, then to confess that Christ is risen is to confess that the last reality is trustworthy and loyal even in death. When such a confession is made among social companions who share Jesus Christ as representative Thou, the vision of the Christian community as a revolutionary movement takes on substance.

RELATIVISM AND THE SOVEREIGNTY OF GOD

As Niebuhr's anthropology derives its coherence from the assumption of relational selfhood, so Niebuhr's theology derives its integrity from the assumption that all persons live and move and have their being in God. The One beyond the many is the constitution of things, the "environment environing all our environments."[1] The struggle among the forms of faith and the universal intent manifest in triadic relations of commitment argue for Niebuhr's brand of religious realism rooted ultimately in the sovereignty of God.

Sometimes the sovereign deity is described in abstract terms such as "principle of being" and "principle of value." At other times the description is deeply personal as when we confront the last reality as void or enemy or companion. There is much in Niebuhr's work that articulates the identity of the transcendent One and the First Person of revelation. But this One we encounter as Thou is also the One *in* the many, the living God active in the complex relational interaction that characterizes our existence as selves. Niebuhr does not hesitate to affirm the immanence of the sovereign God. His understanding of Jesus Christ as symbolic form and his description of universal responsibility as a mode of action that anticipates God's reaction to human behavior indicate the seriousness with which Niebuhr takes the reciprocity of divine-human relations.

Niebuhr's analysis of relational selfhood provides the basis for the identification of divine immanence and divine transcendence in human experience. But there is nothing in Niebuhr's work that explicates that identity in God. Lacking any form of metaphysical inquiry, Niebuhr is open to charges of epistemological dualism on the one hand—there is no analogy between knowledge of selves and knowledge of God—and charges of anthropomorphism on the other—God is limited to a mere reflection or function of human experience.

Niebuhr's failure to undertake metaphysical analysis or point to possible resources for such a program results in an explicit inconsistency that tends to qualify his strong emphasis on the interactive character of the God-human relationship. Clearly Niebuhr does not have a static view of God. In defining his ethics of response against the charge that it is simply resignation to the will of God, Niebuhr speaks of "the loving dynamic One, who does new things," whose relation to the world is "more like that of father to his children than like that of the maker to his manufactures."[2] Yet all the receptivity and responsiveness seems to be on our side of the relationship: ". . . though God's relation to man is not qualified by man's acceptance or rejection of his presence, man's relation to God is evidently so qualified."[3] Nowhere, to my knowledge, does Niebuhr grant that God is in *any* sense conditioned. This, by itself, seriously jeopardizes the I-Thou relation so important in Niebuhr's understanding of revelation. In such a relation both parties are known and are never again quite the same. If this relation and the universal responsibility it empowers are more than poetic expressions, Niebuhr's theology must make explicit some sense in which God is conditioned. We can agree with his claim that the independence of God from experience does not imply God's remoteness from experience unless that independence is absolute in every respect. As it stands, the failure to qualify God's absoluteness tends to undermine the foundation of Niebuhr's position in a responsive God-person relationship.

Metaphysics, as the term is intended here, refers to a comprehensive analysis of the general structures of human experience. Such an analysis is certainly not the heart of theology. Nor can it provide assurance that the One beyond the many is trustworthy, a confidence that reason alone cannot give. In the case of Niebuhr's theology, metaphysics could not claim a certainty contrary to the limitations of relativism. Recognizing these qualifications, there is no more cause to avoid metaphysics as a source of theological insight and a mode of theological expression than there is to avoid the social sciences.

Niebuhr's assertion that radical monotheism dethrones all absolutes short of the principle of being and reverences every relative existent points to the significance of real relations in being, relations that will not yield to the distorted perspectives of exclusive faiths. His understanding of creation and his conversionist view of culture amount to claims that the constitution of the universe really is redemptive. These elements in Niebuhr's work could be strengthened by metaphysical explication. His simultaneous expression of God's absoluteness and relatedness could be clarified through discussions of the sort that are going on in process philosophy.

Process philosophers and theologians have advanced a conception of God that seeks to allow at once for divine absoluteness and relatedness. According to this "dipolar" or "panentheistic" view, God is eternal *and* temporal, necessary *and* contingent, infinite *and* finite, self-sufficient *and* dependent. In each pair of ultimate contraries, both poles are affirmed but with respect to different aspects of God. So, for example, speaking concretely we can describe God as eminently related to the world and in this respect historically dependent. Indeed, in this contingent aspect God is supremely temporal, unsurpassed by any other in the capacity to relate deeply and comprehensively to all existents. But speaking abstractly we can describe God as absolute, in this respect eternally self-sufficient. It is in this aspect that God exists necessarily. To be unsurpassed in this sense is to be ontologically unique.

Panentheism, as the word itself suggests, expresses conceptually the identity of God as the One *in* and *beyond* the many, the First Person in whom we live and move and have our being. The metaphysical approach suggested here, not as a substitute for but as a complement to Niebuhr's theology, restores an analogy between knowledge of selves and knowledge of God and clarifies the sense in which one can speak of God as interactive. Neither dualistic nor anthropomorphic, dipolar theism or panentheism provides additional ways of expressing Niebuhr's universal intent, his global understanding of redemption, his concern for the fate of the earth as well as any individual's destiny.

Metaphysics need not make theology apologetic in the defensive sense Niebuhr seeks to avoid. But does it suggest that God can be known apart from deity value? Certainly if God is sovereign in the strong sense Niebuhr asserts, God can be known apart from deity value, though not as God, that is to say, not as the object of the observer's own ultimate trust and loyalty. Niebuhr grants this himself, and in the case of Jesus Christ he allows for a metaphysical analysis to complement his own examination from the point of view of a moralist. A metaphysician can consider the One in and beyond the many even though that person does not have faith in the God revealed in Jesus Christ. There is certainly nothing in Niebuhr's position to preclude the theologian from undertaking metaphysical studies.

THEOLOGY AND THE PHILOSOPHY OF RELIGION

The metaphysical inquiry suggested above is in line with theology's double task of reasoning in faith and criticizing faith, "not as a subjective attitude or activity only but in relation to its objects."[4] Such an inquiry does not preclude the theologian's own participation in the activity of faith. Rather it accepts the challenge of radical monotheism that Niebuhr's own wide-ranging work so clearly demonstrates. For the radical monotheist trusting in the sovereignty of God, the entire realm of being, and with it all human endeavor, is proper subject matter for theology.

Niebuhr's own exploration of the universal context of relational selfhood is often carried out in the style of a philosopher of religion. Insofar as *The Responsible Self* develops an instrument of analysis applicable to any form of human life, it is moral philosophy. *The Social Sources of Denominationalism* takes a sociological approach to the church in America. *Radical Monotheism and Western Culture*, in its analysis of the forms of faith and the manifestation of those forms in science and politics as well as religion, exhibits the stance of the anthropologist as much as the theologian. In *The Meaning of Revelation* and *Christ and Culture* one is often more aware of Niebuhr the historian than Niebuhr the theologian. A student of religion can profit from Niebuhr's work considered solely as one example of the philosophical, sociological, anthropological, and historical methods of examining the phenomenon called religion.

At the same time, Niebuhr is a Christian theologian. *The Responsible Self* is a Christian moral philosophy because it is written from the standpoint of a follower of Jesus Christ in relation to God. Having written *The Social Sources of Denominationalism*, Niebuhr writes *The Kingdom of God in America* because he is dissatisfied with the sociological account taken by itself. *Radi-*

cal Monotheism and Western Culture, for all its forms of faith
and analyses of culture, includes Niebuhr's own confession that
where he sees radical monotheistic faith he sees Jesus Christ.
The historian of *The Meaning of Revelation* and *Christ and Culture* is finally an apologist for the meaning and power of one
particular event to organize and transform history itself.

Can Niebuhr be a theologian *and* a philosopher of religion?
Can he examine the phenomenon called religion while participating in one of its manifestations? Can the event that continually revolutionizes his own life be the object of his philosophical,
sociological, anthropological, and historical analyses? Can the self-
reflective sophistication of post-Enlightenment humanity be
coupled with the genuine confession that Jesus Christ is a personal disclosure of the last reality as trustworthy and loyal?

These questions are important, not only for individual Christians and students of religion, but for seminaries and college or
university departments of religious studies. These questions are
important for women and men who seek self-understanding and
guidance in an age of rapidly accelerating change, an age in which
even the relativizers are being relativized. These questions are
an invitation to read Niebuhr's work.

SELECTED AND ANNOTATED BIBLIOGRAPHY
OF H. RICHARD NIEBUHR'S WRITINGS
IN CHRONOLOGICAL ORDER

"Back to Benedict?" *Christian Century*, 2 (July 1925), pp. 860–61.
Discussion of monastic ideal as antidote to this-worldliness in Christianity; illustrates Niebuhr's dialectical approach; borders on this-world—other-world dualism.

"Jesus Christ Intercessor." *The International Journal of Religious Education*, 3 (January 1927): 6–8.
Discussion of intercessory prayer and Jesus' role in establishing an intercessory community; how prayer makes a difference to God.

The Social Sources of Denominationalism. New York: Henry Holt and Company, Inc., 1929, 1957.
An examination of the ethical problems of denominationalism from a sociological perspective; describes the class, ethnic, regional, and racial origins of the denominations.

"The Irreligion of Communist and Capitalist." *Christian Century*, 29 October 1930, pp. 1306–7.
Niebuhr sees similarity in approach to religious attitudes, secular outlook, and cynicism between Communist and capitalist.

"Religion and Ethics." *The World Tomorrow*, 13 (November 1930): 443–46.
Points out shortcomings of religion without ethics and ethics without religion; suggests a relation of support within a system of tensions; influence of Kant is apparent.

"Religious Realism in the Twentieth Century." In *Religious Realism*, edited by D. C. MacIntosh, pp. 413–28. New York: The Macmillan Company, 1931.
Historical and epistemological review of term "religious realism"; comparison of Barthian movement and Tillich's theology; call for critical realism.

"The Grace of Doing Nothing." *Christian Century*, 23 March 1932, pp. 378–80.
Analysis of the inactivity of radical Christianity in the conflict between China and Japan.

"The Only Way into the Kingdom of God." *Christian Century*, 6 April 1932, p. 447.
Response to Reinhold Niebuhr's response to "The Grace of Doing Nothing"; comments on God, the structure of the universe, and history.

The Church Against the World. With Wilhelm Pauck and Francis P. Miller. Chicago: Willett, Clark & Company, 1935. "The Question of the Church," pp. 1–13; "Toward the Independence of the Church," pp. 123–56.

Touches on many themes that occupy Niebuhr for the rest of his career as churchman and theologian; emphasis on the need to distinguish the church from the world.

"Man the Sinner." *Journal of Religion*, 15 (July 1935): 272–80.
Doctrine of sin presupposes doctrine of creation; sin the failure to worship God as God; Christian strategy should seek reconciliation and avoid moralism.

The Kingdom of God in America. New York: Harper & Row, Publishers, 1937.
Faith in the kingdom of God used as an interpretive tool to analyze the meaning and movement of American Christianity; the theological companion piece to *The Social Sources of Denominationalism.*

"Value Theory and Theology." In *The Nature of Religious Experience*, edited by J. S. Bixler, R. L. Calhoun, and H. R. Niebuhr, pp. 93–116. New York: Harper & Brothers, Publishers, 1937.
Critique of theological use of value theory in terms of scientific inadequacy, religious inaccuracy, and philosophical dubiety. Niebuhr's own case for objective relativism.

"Life Is Worth Living." *Intercollegian and Far Horizons*, 57 (October 1939): 3–4, 22.
Discussion of faith in relation to the question of life's meaning; understanding of God and Jesus Christ foreshadows Niebuhr's later work in *Radical Monotheism and Western Culture.*

The Meaning of Revelation. New York: The Macmillan Company, 1941.
Examines relativism and analyzes its implications for revelation; describes the God revealed in Jesus Christ and in the permanent revolution that is Christianity.

"The Christian Church in the World's Crisis." *Christianity and Society*, 6 (Summer 1941): 11–17.
Religion provides the context in which particular actions have their meaning and effect; Niebuhr takes the real issue of his time to be that between internationalism and universalism and nationalism.

"War as the Judgment of God." *Christian Century*, 13 May 1942, pp. 630–33.
Interprets God's action in World War II as redemptive and vicarious, absolute, and unified; outlines the consequences of human action.

"Is God in the War?" *Christian Century*, 5 August 1942, pp. 953–55.
Reply to responses to "War as the Judgment of God"; Niebuhr not trying to understand war from God's point of view; further definition of judgment and vicarious suffering.

"War as Crucifixion." *Christian Century*, 28 April 1943, pp. 513–15.
Crucifixion of Jesus Christ as an interpretive image; like the cross, war reveals the order of reality and the graciousness of God.

"A Christian Interpretation of War." Unpublished essay in the possession of James M. Gustafson (1943), 10 pp.
God's action in war and human action in war; conditions for the church's interpretation of war.

"The Ego-Alter Dialectic and the Conscience." *Journal of Philosophy*, 42 (1945): 352–59.
> Self's capacity to be both subject and object rooted in the social context; exploration of ideas developed more fully in *The Responsible Self*.

"The Hidden Church and the Churches in Sight." *Religion in Life*, 15 (Winter 1945–46): 106–16.
> Treatment of the classical contradiction between the church that persons love and the particular religious organizations that go by that name; Niebuhr follows his analysis of several inadequate interpretations with his own understanding of the church as an emergent reality and the churches as subject to continuous conversion.

"The Responsibility of the Church for Society." In *The Gospel, the Church and the World*, edited by Kenneth Scott Latourette, pp. 111–33. New York: Harper & Brothers, Publishers, 1946.
> Christian responsibility "to" and "for" as concepts in understanding the worldly church and the isolated church; discussion of the apostolic, pastoral, and pioneering functions of the Christian community; suggestive of ideas that come to full expression in *Christ and Culture* and *The Responsible Self*.

"Evangelical and Protestant Ethics." In *The Heritage of the Reformation*, edited by E. J. Arndt, pp. 211–29. New York: Richard R. Smith, 1950.
> Critique of Protestant ethics as defensively culture-bound, ecclesiastical, or individualized; Evangelical ethics positively defined as theocentric, faithful, free, and momentary.

Christ and Culture. New York: Harper & Brothers, 1951.
> Using the dialectic of Christ and culture, Niebuhr sets forth a five-fold typology of Christian ethics; rich in historical and theological interpretations, this book offers a comprehensive picture of Jesus Christ.

"The Idea of Covenant and American Democracy." *Church History*, 23 (June 1954): 126–35.
> Discussion of covenant as a pattern that guided persons in the formation of American democracy; significance of covenant as a symbol in ethics, politics, and religion.

"The Triad of Faith." *Andover Newton Bulletin*, 47 (October 1954): 3–12.
> An exploration of the structure of faith as involving trust, loyalty, and a transcending cause; I's and Thou's, Jesus Christ, and God illustrate triad of faith; preview of faith as defined in *Radical Monotheism and Western Culture*.

Christian Ethics. With Waldo Beach. New York: The Ronald Press Company, 1955.
> Niebuhr contributes an "Introduction to Biblical Ethics" (pp. 10–45); he also introduces readings from Martin Luther (pp. 235–43), John Calvin (pp. 267–74), and Jonathan Edwards (pp. 380–89).

The Purpose of the Church and Its Ministry. With Daniel Day Williams and James M. Gustafson. New York: Harper & Brothers, 1956.
> These reflections on the aims of theological education in the mid-50s offer

a polar analysis of the church; the purpose of the church is defined in terms of reconciliation.

"The Church Defines Itself in the World." Unpublished essay in the possession of James M. Gustafson (1957), 15 pp.
Reflective criticism from the standpoint of moral theology on the nature of definition and the contemporary church's effort to define itself; considerable attention to theoretical-practical distinction.

"Martin Luther and the Renewal of Human Confidence." Unpublished address delivered at Valparaiso University (1959), 21 pp.
Faith as the focus of newness in the Reformation and in Luther; exemplifies wedding of interpretation and reality in Niebuhr's theological reflections.

Radical Monotheism and Western Culture. New York: Harper & Brothers, Publishers, 1943, 1952, 1955, 1960.
A thorough analysis of faith as confidence and loyalty and the forms of faith as henotheism, polytheism, and radical monotheism; discussion of relational value theory in "The Center of Value" (pp. 10–13); "Faith in Gods and in God" (pp. 114–26), first written in 1943, responds to question "How is faith in God possible?"

"Reformation, Continuing Imperative." *Christian Century*, 2 March 1960, pp. 248–51.
Niebuhr's entry in *Christian Century* series "How My Mind Has Changed"; his own perspective on major influences, developments, and themes in his work.

"Towards New Symbols." Second of four unpublished Cole Lectures delivered at Vanderbilt University (1960), 30 pp.
Exploration of symbols and their function in various triadic relations; analysis of certain Christian symbols; supplements discussions of symbolic form in *The Responsible Self*.

"On the Nature of Faith." In *Religious Experience and Truth*, edited by Sidney Hook, pp. 93–102. New York: New York University Press, 1961.
Semantic clarification and phenomenological analysis of faith; distinction between Greek and Hebrew meanings; concentration on latter as trust and loyalty.

"Ex Librus." *Christian Century*, 13 June 1961, p. 754.
The ten books that did the most to shape Niebuhr's vocational attitude and philosophy of life.

"The Illusions of Power." *The Pulpit*, 33 (April 1962): 100–103.
Isaiah 10 the text for an interpretation of the cold war between Christendom and communism; word of God and God's work with respect to our power, goodness, and evil and that of our enemy.

The Responsible Self. New York: Harper & Row, Publishers, 1963.
Published posthumously, an essay on moral philosophy that sets forth Niebuhr's theory of responsibility; universal movement implicit in the analysis of selfhood; description of Jesus Christ as symbolic form.

"The Ethical Crisis." *Universitas*, 2 (Spring 1964): 41–50.
   A lecture delivered at Wayne State University in 1961; Protestant diagnosis of our moral illness in terms of our relation to our ultimate environment; importance of grace.

SELECTED SECONDARY SOURCES

Clebsch, William. *American Religious Thought*. Chicago: The University of Chicago Press, 1973.
Understands Niebuhr to have summarized the legacy of American religious thought that runs from Jonathan Edwards to Ralph Waldo Emerson to William James.

Fowler, James W. *To See the Kingdom*. Nashville: Abingdon Press, 1974.
Traces the development of Niebuhr's thought chronologically through his writings; extensive interpretation of work by Niebuhr that remains unpublished and generally unavailable.

Godsey, John D. *The Promise of H. Richard Niebuhr*. Philadelphia: J. B. Lippincott Co., 1970.
A thematic summary of Niebuhr's work; includes a consideration of critical questions frequently posed.

Gustafson, James M. "Introduction." In H. Richard Niebuhr, *The Responsible Self*, pp. 6–41.
Places *The Responsible Self* in the setting of Niebuhr's corpus and the framework of systematic ethics; examines Niebuhr's understanding of our response to God as Creator, Governor, and Redeemer.

Kliever, Lonnie. *H. Richard Niebuhr*. Waco, Texas: Word Books, Publisher, 1977.
Treats Niebuhr as reformer, theologian, and ethicist; considers the ambiguities in Niebuhr's thought as well as its contemporary relevance.

Ramsey, Paul, ed. *Faith and Ethics*. New York: Harper & Brothers, 1957.
A collection of critical essays written by Niebuhr's colleagues at Yale University and elsewhere; two contributions by Hans W. Frei deal with the development of Niebuhr's thought and the primary influences upon it.

Fuller bibliographies of Niebuhr's writings and secondary sources appear in Fowler, *To See the Kingdom*, and Ramsey, *Faith and Ethics*.

NOTES

Introduction

1. John D. Godsey, *The Promise of H. Richard Niebuhr* (Philadelphia: J. B. Lippincott Company, 1970), p. 14.

Chapter I.

1. H. Richard Niebuhr, *The Responsible Self* (New York: Harper & Row, Publishers, 1963), p. 56. Hereafter cited as *RS*.
2. *Ibid.*, p. 71.
3. *Ibid.*, p. 78.
4. *Ibid.*, p. 79.
5. *Ibid.*
6. *Ibid.*, p. 85.
7. H. Richard Niebuhr, "Life Is Worth Living," *Intercollegian and Far Horizons*, 57 (October 1939): 22.
8. *RS*, p. 65.
9. *Ibid.*, p. 46.
10. *Ibid.*, p. 60.
11 *Ibid.*, p. 64.
12. H. Richard Niebuhr, *Radical Monotheism and Western Culture* (New York: Harper & Brothers, Publishers, 1943, 1952, 1955, 1960), p. 16. Hereafter cited as *RMWC*.
13. H. Richard Niebuhr, "The Triad of Faith," *Andover Newton Bulletin*, 47 (October 1954): 8.
14. *RMWC*, p. 23.
15. *Ibid.*, p. 119.
16. *Ibid.*, p. 34.
17. *Ibid.*, p. 33.
18. *Ibid.*, p. 40.
19. *Ibid.*, p. 69.
20. *Ibid.*, p. 37.

Chapter II.

1. H. Richard Niebuhr, *The Meaning of Revelation* (New York: The Macmillan Company, 1941), p. 7. Hereafter cited as *MR*.
2. *Ibid.*, p. 10.
3. *RS*, p. 152.
4. *Ibid.*, p. 67.
5. *MR*, p. 13

6. H. Richard Niebuhr, "Toward New Symbols," unpublished Cole Lecture, No. II, delivered at Vanderbilt University, 1961, p. 7.
7. H. Richard Niebuhr, "Reformation: Continuing Imperative," *Christian Century*, 2 March 1960, p. 249.
8. *MR*, p. 22.
9. *Ibid.*, p. 23.
10. *RWMC*, p. 115.
11. Helmut Richard Niebuhr, "Religious Realism in the Twentieth Century," *Religious Realism*, ed. by D. C. MacIntosh (New York: The Macmillan Company, 1931), pp. 413–28.
12. *MR*, p. 48.
13. *Ibid.*, pp. 60–61.
14. *Ibid.*, p. 77.
15. *Ibid.*, p. 99.
16. *Ibid.*, p. 93.
17. *Ibid.*, p. 139.
18. H. Richard Niebuhr, *Christ and Culture*, (New York: Harper & Brothers, 1951), p. 12. Hereafter cited as *CC*.
19. *RS*, p. 43.
20. *CC*, p. 16.
21. *Ibid.*
22. *Ibid.*, p. 17.
23. *Ibid.*, p. 18.
24. *Ibid.*, p. 28.
25. *Ibid.*, p. 19.
26. *Ibid.*, p. 22.
27. *Ibid.*, p. 26.
28. *Ibid.*, p. 25.
29. *Ibid.*, p. 26.
30. *Ibid.*, p. 27.
31. *Ibid.*, p. 29.
32. *Ibid.*
33. *Ibid.*
34. *Andover Newton Bulletin*, 47 (October 1954): 9, 10.
35. *RS*, p. 167.
36. *Ibid.*, p. 154.
37. *Ibid.*, p. 155.
38. *Ibid.*, p. 163.
39. *MR*, p. 147.
40. *Ibid.*, pp. 151–52.
41. *Ibid.*, pp. 152, 153.
42. *RMWC*, pp. 121–22.
43. *Ibid.*, p. 122.
44. *Ibid.*
45. *Ibid.*, pp. 123–24.
46. *Christian Century*, 2 March 1960, p. 249.
47. *RS*, pp. 175–76.
48. *Ibid.*, p. 176.
49. *Ibid.*, p. 143.

Notes 119

CHAPTER III.

1. Waldo Beach and H. Richard Niebuhr, *Christian Ethics* (New York: The Ronald Press Company, 1955), p. 33.
2. *RMWC*, p. 37.
3. *Ibid.*, p. 42.
4. *RS*, p. 122.
5. *Ibid.*, pp. 123–24.
6. H. Richard Niebuhr, *The Kingdom of God in America* (New York: Harper & Row, Publishers, Incorporated, 1937), p. 51.
7. *RMWC*, p. 47.
8. *Christian Ethics*, p. 18.
9. *MR*, p. 140.
10. *RS*, p. 120.
11. *Christian Ethics*, p. 36.
12. *MR*, p. 185.
13. *Ibid.*, p. 187.
14. *Ibid.*, p. 190.
15. H. Richard Niebuhr, "Man the Sinner," *Journal of Religion*, 15 (July 1935): 278.
16. *Ibid.*, p. 277.
17. *RS*, p. 142.
18. H. Richard Niebuhr, "Martin Luther and the Renewal of Human Confidence," unpublished address delivered at Valparaiso University, 1959, p. 18.
19. *Journal of Religion*, 15 (July 1935): 273.
20. *CC*, p. 193.
21. *Ibid.*, p. 199.
22. H. Richard Niebuhr, "Is God in the War?", *Christian Century*, 5 August 1942, p. 954.
23. *RS*, p. 125.
24. H. Richard Niebuhr, "A Christian Interpretation of War," unpublished essay in the possession of James M. Gustafson (1943), p. 2.
25. H. Richard Niebuhr, "War as the Judgment of God," *Christian Century*, 13 May 1942, p. 631.
26. "A Christian Interpretation of War," p. 6
27 H. Richard Niebuhr, "War as Crucifixion," *Christian Century*, 28 April 1943, p. 515.
28. "A Christian Interpretation of War," p. 7.
29. *Ibid.*, p. 8.
30. *Christian Century*, 5 August 1942, p. 954.
31. *Ibid.*
32. *Christian Century*, 13 May 1942, p. 631.

CHAPTER IV.

1. *RS*, p. 143.
2. *RMWC*, p. 118.
3. *Christian Century*, 2 March 1960, p. 251.
4. See *RMWC*, pp. 49–63.
5. *CC*, p. 11.

6. *RMWC*, p. 58.
7. H. Richard Niebuhr, *The Purpose of the Church and Its Ministry* (New York: Harper & Brothers, 1956), p. 19. See pp. 17–27 for Niebuhr's polar analysis.
8. *The Kingdom of God in America*, p. 67.
9. *Christian Century*, 2 March 1960, p. 249.
10. H. Richard Niebuhr, "The Hidden Church and the Churches in Sight," *Religion in Life*, 15 (Winter 1945–46): 114.
11. H. Richard Niebuhr, "The Church Defines Itself in the World," unpublished essay in the possession of James M. Gustafson (1957), p. 5.
12. *Ibid.*, p. 7.
13. H. Richard Niebuhr, "Back to Benedict?" *Christian Century*, 2 July 1925, p. 860.
14. H. Richard Niebuhr, et al., *The Church Against the World* (Chicago: Willett, Clark & Company, 1935), pp. 128–39.
15. H. Richard Niebuhr, "The Responsibility of the Church for Society," in *The Gospel, the Church and the World*, ed. Kenneth Scott Latourette (New York: Harper & Brothers, Publishers, 1946), pp. 120–26.
16. "The Church Defines Itself in the World," p. 5.
17. *Christian Century*, 2 March 1960, p. 250.
18. *The Church Against the World*, p. 124.
19. *Ibid.*, p. 11.
20. See H. Richard Niebuhr, "Religion and Ethics," *The World Tomorrow*, 13 (November 1930): 443–46.
21. H. Richard Niebuhr, "Evangelical and Protestant Ethics," in *The Heritage of the Reformation: Essays Commemorating the Centennial of Eden Theological Seminary*, ed. E. J. F. Arndt (New York: Richard R. Smith, 1950), p. 219.
22. *Ibid.*, p. 220.
23. *Ibid.*, p. 222.
24. *Ibid.*
25. *Ibid.*, p. 223.
26. *Ibid.*
27. *Ibid.*, p. 224.
28. *Ibid.*, pp. 225–26.
29. *Ibid.*, p. 227.
30. H. Richard Niebuhr, "The Christian Church in the World Crisis," *Christianity and Society*, 6 (Summer 1941): 16.
31. H. Richard Niebuhr, "The Ethical Crisis," *Universitas* 2 (Spring 1964): 49–50.
32. *The Purpose of the Church and Its Ministry*.
33. *The Gospel, the Church and the World*, p. 118.
34. *Ibid.*, pp. 118–19.
35. *Ibid.*, p. 121.
36. *Ibid.*, p. 122.
37. *Ibid.*, p. 124.
38. *Ibid.*, p. 126.
39. *Ibid.*, p. 128.
40. *Ibid.*, pp. 128–29.

41. *Ibid.*, p. 129.
42. *Ibid.*, p. 132.

CONCLUSION
  1. *RS*, p. 175.
  2. *RS*, p. 173.
  3. *Ibid.*, p. 44.
  4. *RMWC*, p. 15